OUTPACER

OUTPACER

By Alex Holt

The blueprint for breakthrough success in the digital era

1

Published in 2022 by Ebury Edge an imprint of Ebury Publishing,
20 Vauxhall Bridge Road,
London SW1V 2SA

Ebury Edge is part of the Penguin Random House group of companies
whose addresses can be found at global.penguinrandomhouse.com

The views and ideas of the author as expressed in this book are entirely his own.
The book is not endorsed by or associated with KPMG LLP or any of its affiliates.

This edition first published by Ebury Edge in 2022

www.penguin.co.uk

A CIP catalogue record for this book is available from the British Library

Hardback ISBN: 9781529146134
Trade Paperback ISBN: 9781529146141

Printed and bound in Great Britain by Clays Ltd, Elcograf S.p.A.

The authorised representative in the EEA is Penguin Random House Ireland,
Morrison Chambers, 32 Nassau Street, Dublin D02 YH68

For Natalie, Leo and Bailey

CONTENTS

OUTPACER

They are the disrupters.

The ones shattering the models and myths we live by.

The ones who wake up every day and change how we live, work, play and communicate.

They don't dust off old tools for new problems.

They build new tools to solve them.

They don't float in the mainstream.

They navigate the waves of unremitting change.

Not just imagining, but out-imagining.

Not just performing, but out-performing.

Not just keeping pace, but outpacing.

Welcome to the era of the Outpacer.

INTRODUCTION

We all know who *they* are – the organizations with ambitious visions and disruptive models that seem to glide effortlessly through the new digital economy, achieving astonishing earnings, customer growth rates and market share gains time and time again.

More often than not, they shape the markets they choose to operate in and dictate the pace of change. They are engaging and iconic, with customers who act more like fans than consumers.

Over the past decade we have seen a small number of companies changing every aspect of how we live, work and play. They have created incredible businesses that have redefined what a successful organization looks and feels like. For example, let's reflect on the performance of what Jim Cramer called the "Faangs" (Facebook, Amazon, Apple, Netflix, Google), which have added $8 trillion in share values since 2013. Year in, year out, quarter after quarter, they deliver incredible growth and value for investors.

On the whole, leaders of any Technology, Media and Telecoms (TMT) business are typically very bright individuals who are high achievers. The challenge for leaders in TMT businesses that are not delivering performances like that of the "Faangs" is the incredibly high benchmark that is already in everyone's mind. It begs the question, from a variety of sources, including themselves: "If they can do it, why can't you?"

I'm lucky to have an amazing job. I meet, work with and get to know the leaders of the world's top TMT companies. At its core, my job requires me to understand the challenges these leaders face today and tomorrow and, importantly, the opportunities that are available to them to enhance the overall performance of the organization they lead.

Sometimes it's an unwelcome intervention to force change, but at its best, it means working with a team to take on a new challenge, often where there is a meeting of minds on purpose, values, goals and execution, plus a lively debate on how to get there. Over more than twenty years I've had the privilege of an inside view of how the TMT industry has evolved and what it takes to outpace all in sight.

A few years back I had a meeting with a CEO of a multi-billion dollar TMT company. We'd spent time discussing a number of options for a new strategy. All went well, but at the end, the CEO turned to me and said, "How do *they* do it?"

"Who?" I asked.

"*Them.*"

This CEO didn't even have a name for them, but meant the pacesetters in digital.

"Quarter after quarter *they* make it look easy."

But it wasn't just this CEO who was searching for an answer to that question. I reflected on other conversations and the fervor I'd observed when an insight was shared by one of "*them*" on how they ran their business. As soon as I walked out of the room, I knew I needed to find the answer. That's why over the last few years I've combined research and personal experiences to identify the "secrets" to the Outpacers' success.

Running a business is the ultimate non-athletic competitive endeavor. You and all your stakeholders are constantly comparing every aspect of performance to the leading marker. Looking at the

S&P 500 or FTSE 100 over the past thirty years, there have always been those businesses out in front and leading the way. But for those following, the gap has never been so seemingly insurmountable as it appears today.

As we approached the end of the second digital decade, that gap was growing, and then as we went into the 2020s, the impact of Covid-19 turned that gap from a lead to a chasm. So much so, in fact, that the alleged dominance of these tech goliaths has caught the attention of the global competition authorities.

So does this signal a white flag from the competition? Is it game over? Time for the rest to throw in the towel? Well, not from where I'm standing. We are in the midst of the fourth industrial revolution. Change is everywhere and many have now accepted the view of author Marshall Goldsmith that "what got you here won't get you there". If you're not currently at the front of the race, it's not the time to roll over. It's time to find out how to grab a piece of this new digital action.

Over the course of this book I'm going to share three key components to help your organization become an Outpacer or continue to perform as one. I'll take you through the nine characteristics that underpin the success of an Outpacer. If you were a sports coach, you'd describe it as your system. But just like in sports, it takes far more than a system to create championship-winning teams. I'll spotlight the individuals that exemplify the Outpacer characteristics in the incredible businesses they lead. By understanding the system, the organizations and the archetypal businesspeople, you'll discover the inner workings of the Outpacers.

But I didn't want to stop there. One thing I'll share with you right now is that Outpacers have a fair amount of healthy paranoia. Typically, they disrupted something to create their business and they are always looking over their shoulder to make sure they're not being complacent about their own trajectory. They also tend to be intellectually curious, open to (polite) criticism and different points of view that help them to find that extra edge. So I've gone further than the business leaders that lead in digital, to look at how non-corporate popular icons have achieved greatness and what we can all learn from them.

I'm a big believer in looking outside of your environment to learn new ways of doing things. If you're running a business, all of the following are important as you lead in the digital era: followship, influencing millions, being respected, having an impact, creating a desire to engage with you, changing behavior and inspiring action. Not many CEOs know they do this day in and day out. But if you're one of a handful of popular icons, this is what you do, and today's business leaders have a lot to learn from how these Outpacers have created a formula for impeccable leadership in our digital lives.

The leaders of the Outpacers are finding that it's not just corporate and business matters their employees want them to be leaders on. With religion playing a decreasing role in many people's lives and large swathes of society in total despair with the political establishment, many are looking to their corporate leaders for inspiration and purpose and to take a leading role on social issues. Oh, and they need to get it right – every time.

Why the crossover of popular icons and business greats? Well, if there's one thing we've learnt from Covid, it's that there's no real work–life balance. It's more about achieving a healthy work–life blend. The crossover between work and life has never been more prominent and never more important to harnessing the power of an organization's true potential.

So as you finish each chapter, you'll find a profile of a business icon and a popular icon. Each one has been hand-picked by me because of the inspiration they've given me and the lessons I think you can learn from them. Think of them as the people I'd invite to my Outpacer dinner party. I'm hosting and you get to join us. It's going to be fantastic, so sit back and enjoy.

CHAPTER 1

CLEAR VISION AND MISSION – THE mVISION

In today's cut-throat environment, there is a war for customers and a war for talent. The power of a clear vision and mission in attracting talent and customers is undeniable. Too often, both the mission and vision are cobbled together at an off-site by "leadership" or, worse still, given to third-parties to write. Frequently they're bland, uninspiring and, quite frankly, cringeworthy!

One thing that sets an Outpacer apart from the rest of the field is the store they set by their epic mission and vision. Sometimes at first glance they seem glib, as if someone just wrote down the first thing that came into their head, for example, "organize the world's information". Surely, to be a trillion-dollar business, doesn't it need to be a bit more complicated?

The answer is no. The ability of Outpacers to set out a clear direction of travel that's simple to articulate, that everyone is on board with, that is going to achieve incredible outcomes and delight a variety of stakeholders, is part of their magic.

The mVision: What does this really mean?

The organization understands what it wants to be in the future and has a clear plan for how to achieve it. The mission and vision are clear, ambitious and easily articulated, and they gel together seamlessly. When you get that combination just right – I call it the mVision – there is a perfect flow between the mission and vision, values, strategy and goals, that in turn leads to well-defined and compelling customer propositions.

Leadership continuously communicates and reinforces the mVision to stakeholders and employees. Most importantly, the mVision is viewed by all stakeholders as purposeful; it is a driving force motivating and demanding the very best from everyone, every day.

Why is this important?

An Outpacer redefines the world around them. They have a higher purpose and clearly understand how they intend to change the lives of millions or even billions. Outpacers are empowered by a strong mission and vision. They take risks and will make big investments to achieve their aims. They have clarity on the short-, medium- and long-term priorities. That balance is clear because the mission and vision flow together and define priorities. The Outpacer has employees who are more engaged, with customers who are like loyal fans, and they are prepared to take bigger risks in the pursuit of the mVision.

Outpacers get the right talent brought into all the components of the mVision; the vision, mission, values, strategy and goals create a sense of ownership and passion for its execution so that everything else starts to fall into place. The mVision doesn't mean you can go into full auto-pilot, but getting it right is a bit like having the lane warning sensors on in your car. It helps everyone to stay in their lane en route to their dream destination.

Mission power

When JFK announced in 1961 that the US "should commit itself to achieving the goal, before this decade is out, of landing a man on the Moon and returning him safely to the Earth", the idea was truly audacious. To put things into perspective, an iPhone has more processing power than every NASA computer in existence had at that time. Over the course of the following eight years, the 400,000 employees at NASA would need to pull together to achieve the entire mission, from the rocket and the spacesuits to how to ensure that the stars and stripes flag was able to fly on the moon. One of the overwhelming reasons for success was the clarity of the vision and mission. Everyone knew exactly what the goal was – to get a man to the moon and back – and that the mission was time-bound – by the end of the decade. Through their incredible purposeful intent, JFK's words captured the imagination of NASA, the United States and much of the world. It's an excellent example of the power of a vision and mission working together to inspire. Over fifty years later, technology has moved on exponentially, but the extraordinary power of words remains the same. It's something Outpacers know only too well, as we'll see.

The mVision

The difference between visions, missions, and strategy is often misunderstood, and when values and goals get thrown into the mix, there is even greater confusion. Each is a different component of what I think of as a powerful communications tool – the mVision. When done well, the five elements work together in harmony, complementing each other, with a superpower to motivate and inspire.

Let's break down the mVision into five chunks:

1. The vision statement provides inspiration and guidance on where the organization is going in the future. It is a five- to ten-year long-term view that is nothing short of awe inspiring!
2. The mission describes in more immediate terms what you do, who you do it for and why. It explains what's happening today and over the next one to three years. It is the short- and medium-term purpose of the organization and lays out what has to happen to ensure delivery of the vision.
3. Your values define *how* you will pursue the vision and mission, providing clear guidance on the right way to operate and how you and your team should behave. The values connect directly to the chosen strategy and associated goals.
4. Your strategies describe how you plan to achieve the mission, the steps you'll take and the resources that you'll use to do it.
5. Goals are the simple and specific statements of what you need to do and by when to deliver those strategies.

It's relatively easy to write down and explain the five components and their roles. It's another thing to weave them together in perfect harmony and give someone goosebumps when they read it.

Harmony and flow

A great mVision has the power to inspire and motivate, often because those in the organization truly believe in it and its greater purpose. Famously, the story goes that when JFK was visiting the NASA headquarters he introduced himself to a janitor who was mopping the floor and asked him what he did at NASA. "I'm helping put a man on the moon!" said the janitor. The tale became legendary: a perfect example of an mVision providing a purpose for the organization and all the individuals within pursuing it in unison.

But what is less well known is that this vision was born from a challenge that Kennedy set his team. Against the backdrop of the Cold War and the Bay of Pigs fiasco, JFK asked his team to consider various missions that they could beat the Russians at, including a trip around the moon, or a rocket to go to the moon and back with a man. In a letter to the Vice President, leading aerospace engineer Wernher von Braun responded by advising, "We have a sporting chance of sending a three-man crew around the moon ahead of the Soviets. However, the Soviets could conduct a round-the-moon voyage earlier if they are ready to waive certain emergency safety features." However, he continued, "We have an excellent chance of beating the Soviets to the first landing of a crew on the moon (including return capability, of course)". Through a classic strategic rationale, the team looked at the weaknesses of the Russians and at their own strengths and values and suggested the first manned mission to the moon. If you think about the harmony and flow between the vision, mission, values, strategy and goals, it's a great example of an mVision.

Here are some more recent examples. See how the vision provides that long-term, inspiring picture, while the mission provides the shorter-term, more immediate day-to-day instruction.

Apple:

— Vision: We believe that we are on the face of the earth to make great products and that's not changing. We are here to make the best products on earth and to leave the world better than we found it.

— Mission: The company is committed to bringing the best user experience to its customers through its innovative hardware, software and services.

Facebook (Since October 2021 known as Meta, the parent company name for Facebook):

— Vision: To become a privacy-focused messaging and social networking platform where people can communicate securely.

— Mission: To give people the power to build community and bring the world closer together.

Netflix:

— Vision: To become the best global entertainment distribution service, licensing entertainment content around the world, creating markets that are accessible to film makers and helping content creators around the world to find a global audience.

— Mission: We promise our customers stellar service, our suppliers a valuable partner, our investors the prospect of sustained profitable growth and our employees the allure of huge impact.

Microsoft:

— Vision: To help people and businesses throughout the world realize their full potential.

— Mission: To empower every person and every organization on the planet to achieve more.

Getting the balance right

One of the hardest things to do in any business is to get the balance between the short-term imperatives and the longer-term vision. That's why the mVision is so important to get right. It sets out the imperatives showing how today's actions lead to an outpacing future.

Everyone in the organization has a role to play in getting the balance right. When there's an urgency about what everyone is doing and surplus opportunity, getting distracted is easy. It's also easy to do a very long day and believe you're working hard. Sometimes, less is more and you need to ensure the whole organization is working hard **and** smart.

While everyone has a role, leadership is responsible for balance, and it goes right to the top of the house, to the CEO. They make the decisions on the strategies, goals and objectives that will help the organization to reach the promised land! They are the head chef in the kitchen and need to ensure that the team uses the right ingredients (without missing any out) in the right quantities at the right time to create the perfect dish. Everyone needs to know who's doing what, so that they can collaborate and support each other. There needs to be transparency on roles, objectives and goals, with everyone constantly ensuring that they're making the mission happen daily, while en route to delivering the lofty vision that inspires everyone.

In a start-up the team will meet to track progress multiple times in a single day, probably first thing, at lunchtime and at the end of the day. The strategies and goals are challenged constantly and everyone knows exactly who's doing what and why. As organizations get bigger, the check-points often become less frequent – weekly, then monthly – potentially losing much of the transparency and monitoring that's so important.

At Google, everyone's objectives are open to every other Googler and they hold a weekly all-hands meeting to share progress and update everyone. They have held on to some of that start-up ethos and it's critical to them continuing to outpace.

Investors

As a long-term industry player and observer, it is my firm opinion that the pressure of short-term quarterly earnings on publicly listed businesses has prevented many from fulfilling their value potential by causing them to lose sight of, or never really commit to, a compelling mVision.

Investors are clearly extremely important, but they don't all share the same values and they certainly don't share the same objectives as each other. Often they don't have your insights, risk appetite or desire to achieve the mVision. That can quickly become a problem, so getting the right investors is critical.

Many of today's Outpacers take great pleasure in being non-traditional corporate organizations. They are not a slave to traditional wisdom. Instead they set their own rules and have a firm belief in themselves, their teams and their mVision. They often have no fear of failing and stubbornly refuse to be trapped or beholden to analysts and investors who don't have their long-term commitment to seeing the mVision through to reality.

When an Outpacer goes public, it must resist overly short-term pressure from the investor community. You could even go as far as to say that to be an Outpacer you need what traditional executives might consider as a rebellious attitude to the investor community, but it simply comes from an incredible conviction and belief in the mVision.

If you were going to sum up the attitude, it would perhaps be: "Hey, we're happy you've invested (you're also lucky to be on our rocket-ship). Leave us to run the business and we'll let you know how we're getting on. We'll answer your questions if we feel they're worth answering. Just don't tell us what to do. Oh, and we hope you enjoy the ride."

Just look at Amazon founder Jeff Bezos's letter to investors. He wouldn't exactly say the above, but every quarter there's a slightly more formal reminder: "We will continue to make investment decisions in light of long-term market leadership considerations rather than short-term profitability considerations or short-term Wall Street reactions."

However, returning to the point on balance, you can't just blatantly ignore your investors! They are critical stakeholders that you need on board and may have valuable ideas that are worthy of consideration. Getting the right balance means ensuring that you're steering the ship, not them. Use the mVision to get the right investors on board and tell the rest to walk the plank!

What can we learn from today's Outpacers?

UBIQUITOUS PRODUCTS

Some of the most obvious current Outpacers can map their early and current success to the pursuit of an mVision that has led them to develop a ubiquitous product:

Facebook – where everyone goes to connect to everyone.
Amazon – where everyone goes to buy anything.
Apple – where everyone can use accessible technology.
Netflix – where everyone goes to watch everything.
Google – where everyone goes to find information.

These are simple product visions, but in order to achieve them, the product has to be excellent enough for everyone to want to use it. That focus meant that these companies prioritized growth over revenue in the early years. They all had a solid and unshakeable belief in their mVision and were confident they would create a product that people would love, which they could then make profitable.

Take Facebook and Google, who both created a brilliant product in line with their mVision, before thinking about revenue. They recognized that if their products were appealing and attractive to an enormous amount of people, they would have the foundations for creating huge revenue. They created products that were almost ubiquitously attractive; everyone wants to have information at their fingertips, as well as being connected to all of their friends. They then turned to advertising as the most elegant, efficient and ultimately profitable source of income. In business terms this was a no-brainer; however, it was also consistent with their overall mission. Remember Facebook's stated mission is "to give people the power to build community and bring the world closer together".

Zuckerberg argues that his advertising strategy is consistent with that mission: "I believe everyone should have a voice and be able to connect. If we're committed to serving everyone, then we need a service that is affordable to everyone. The best way to do that is to offer services for free, which ads enable us to do."

FORGET CONVENTIONAL WISDOM

We discussed the mission to the moon earlier, but there are a multitude of examples of individuals who would not let conventional thinking hold them back. Whether they were the earliest explorers proving the world wasn't flat, athletes breaking the "impossible" four-minute mile or social justice leaders like Martin Luther King who dared to dream about equality, we have their bravery to thank for progress that otherwise wouldn't have happened, certainly not as soon as it did. I believe that an Outpacer has to have a healthy disdain for conventional thinking, as long as it's in line with the mVision.

Outpacers often use what, at the time, appear to be counterintuitive strategies – and certainly strategies that fly in the face of conventional business wisdom – but are consistent with the mVision. For example, Amazon took the decision to include bad reviews next to products. Ultimately this made Amazon a better place to buy products as it gave customers significantly greater product information than they would (at the time) receive in a conventional store. Similarly, as part of Google's ambition to have the best and most comprehensive search results system, they would include links to competing major search engines such as AskJeeves and Yahoo at the bottom of their page. None of this followed the normal business playbook, but it became critical to their success.

DISCIPLINED DIVERSIFICATION

Mastery of a product followed by disciplined diversification that is consistent with the original mVision is key to achieving hyper-scale as an Outpacer: Apple introduced the iPod, the iPhone and then the iPad to the market with extraordinary success. As with the iPod and the iPad, and now to an extent the iPhone, the market has matured beyond the high-growth phase. But the enormous revenues that these original products generated have been used to fund forays into new markets.

Apple moved successfully into subscription-based service industries, but maintained its mVision, with a focus on simple and well-designed user interfaces. This guides all of the design and engineering of their services like Apple TV+ or Apple News.

Netflix sought the best way to remove friction in consuming entertainment without owning it. They saw, ahead of the curve, that this would become based on streaming and have been the dominant player since. They sought to grow their DVD-based subscription before becoming a technology company that pioneered streaming entertainment and achieved true product mastery with award-winning films and TV series.

Google wanted to create a platform to access all the world's online information. This was then improved with advanced search technologies and elements of personalization when it came to ads and search results. It now operates within Alphabet, alongside a vast range of online services and platforms that include YouTube, Gmail and Android. Thus, despite diversification, the strategy and overall mVision have been consistently executed with great discipline.

Amazon built their e-commerce empire before moving into cloud computing. AWS (Amazon Web Services) is now responsible for two thirds of Amazon's profits – £13.5 billion in 2020. While cloud computing and e-commerce are not seemingly natural bedfellows, the incredible success of AWS has come from following the original vision and mission set out by Jeff Bezos to offer a low price structure based on usage rather than flat fees, which has made it highly appealing to both large and small organizations around the world. It's a great example of disciplined (and hugely successful) diversification.

Strategy is often defined by what you don't do. This is obviously hard to document given that these are events that haven't happened, but we only have to look at various rumors (like an actual Apple TV or Apple car), or think about the plethora of diversification opportunities that present themselves every day, to know that today's Outpacers are very disciplined in saying "no" to an awful lot of things.

These Outpacers have not fallen into the trap of getting complacent. The visions and missions set out by their founders have constantly acted like a personal trainer pushing them and their teams beyond their current limits, motivating and inspiring them to deliver to the highest standards. What sets them apart is that they have all remained focused on the founding vision and mission that created their original success. They've then consistently flowed the vision and mission, in line with the values, to the strategy and the goals. This is the epitome of the mVision.

So how to do it?

We've described the need for harmony and flow between the vision, mission, values, strategy and goals to create an mVision. We've also talked about getting the balance right so that you're delivering every day without losing sight of the bigger picture. Finally, we talked about investors, their importance and the damage they can do if you have the wrong ones. So, now let's move from looking at what an mVision is, to how you create something truly inspiring.

In simple terms, there are four descriptors that need to be present in what you create:

EPIC

There's no room to be bashful! When someone reads your words, they should awaken the senses and give them goosebumps. What you create has to be brave and audacious, so much so that they take a deep breath and think, "WOW, that is truly epic!"

One of the reasons I like the word "epic" is that it conjures up images of excitement, adventure, challenge, scale and a level of difficulty. You need all of these elements throughout your vision, mission, values, strategies and goals to create the kind of motivation and desire you need in your audience.

You've got to come up with something pretty special to ensure that when the alarm goes off for one of your team at 5am, your mVision will be enough to stop them hitting the snooze button and instead get out of bed and bring their best.

Not everyone needs to think it's epic. It doesn't need to appeal to all, but it does need to blow the socks off the talent you want working on your mVision, the customers you're going to be targeting, and investors you want on board.

EXCITEMENT
ADVENTURE
CHALLENGE **= EPIC**
SCALE
DIFFICULTY

While the Outpacers make it look pretty easy to create an epic or audacious vision and mission, the reality is that creating something that motivates employees, customers and key stakeholders is actually very hard. Testing it with people who will honestly tell you if it's epic is key to your Outpacer trajectory, so it's important to create a safe environment where your stakeholders can speak up and tell you what you need to hear. People who tell you what they think you want to hear have no value on your journey.

Google is a great example of the epic mVision:

— Vision: To provide access to the world's information in one click.
— Mission: To organize the world's information and make it universally accessible and useful.

Google Maps is a great example of something that everyone thought was unachievable, which means it fitted well into the epic criteria.

Maps started out as an ambition to simplify how to get from point A to point B. While Google is and was first and foremost a search engine, Maps falls perfectly into its wider mission to organize the world's information and make it universally accessible and useful. After all, maps are simply representations of geographic information.

But physical maps are annoying. They are only as current as the date on which they are printed, and they are virtually impossible to read if you're driving. So this was a perfect venture for Google to get involved with, something that fell perfectly in line with its wider mission.

Google wasn't the first to notice this opportunity. Yahoo! Maps offered a web-based map from 1998 and MapQuest offered turn-by-turn directions. But Google believed it could make a superior product, and when brothers Lars and Jens Rasmussen pitched their nascent project to offer a great web-based map to customers with their start-up, Where 2 Technologies, Google went for it. It acquired the company in October 2004 and this, combined with two further acquisitions, gave it the foundational aspects and technologies needed to create an advanced program that would blow away the competition.

One way in which Google thought it could create a product that would be superior to any already on offer, and stay true to its mission of organizing the whole world's information, was to map it all. As John Hanke, the co-founder of Keyhole and former head of Google's geo-spatial division, told the *Guardian*, "At the time satellite imagery was quite expensive to acquire and scarce because there weren't that many satellites available. I went to show Sergey on the map all the major cities we wanted to acquire. He looked and he just said, 'Why don't we do all of it?' "

Today Google covers 99 per cent of the Earth, with 25 million updates every day, which is probably why there are one billion monthly active users enjoying such a comprehensive, detailed and interactive tool. The mobile app completely blows away the competition, dwarfing the next biggest competitor with six times its market customer share. Google Maps now accounts for around $4 billion in revenues, although Morgan Stanley analyst Brian Nowack commented that it is the "most under-monetized asset" at Google.

PURPOSEFUL

I think it's really important to take a moment to reflect on the importance of purpose in today's world and the role it plays in all our lives, particularly in the companies for whom the best talent in the world chooses to work. One of the best ways to bring it to life is to look at the first Microsoft vision statement from forty years ago. It's often lauded as one of the best vision statements, but in my opinion, it's the lack of purpose within it that dates it.

> "A computer on every desk and in every home."
> **Bill Gates, Microsoft chairman and CEO, 1980**

The psychological power of purpose, and the devastating consequences for those who lose it, cannot be underestimated. Expert psychologists (like my wife) will tell you that the need for purpose is at the core of every human. For a leader, it's one of the keys to true followship. A group of individuals delivering on what they believe to be a purposeful mission can find true fulfillment. Keep that mission going and you lock in that elusive and wonderful feeling of a purposeful and fulfilled existence. And it's key to being an Outpacer.

There is no doubt in my mind that over the last few decades many have been looking beyond traditional religion for purpose, and they are also finding political leadership unable to drive a real sense of purpose in their life. As I was sitting in Silicon Valley on Covid-19 lockdown at the tumultuous end of President Trump's final months in office, it was clear to me that many employees in the world's most dominant businesses wanted and demanded that their corporate leaders stepped into the void and delivered purposeful leadership on social injustice, the environment and democracy.

While many will argue about whether this was done well or not, for me one thing is certain: this was a real moment when the role and responsibility of the leaders of an Outpacer transcended anything we'd seen before in corporate life. There is a pressure and demand from top talent for the leaders of the organizations in which they work to have a moral compass on key topics. To lead an Outpacer, you must also be admired and respected on issues beyond the boardroom.

Let's go back to Microsoft and see how today, under CEO Satya Nadella, purpose has been woven into its vision and mission statement:

Vision: To help people and businesses throughout the world realize their full potential.

Mission: To empower every person and every organization on the planet to achieve more.

When Nadella compared today's statements with the founding vision, he said, "Gates's goal was one with an easily identifiable end point, which didn't foresee the direction the company would take once every home had a computer in it." Since being at the helm, Nadella says he has tried to view Microsoft's new ventures with a culture focus. "Any decision about a new product or a new hire, I'm always thinking about that sense of purpose and culture."

That purpose that Nadella describes is critical to Microsoft's success. It also tells you a lot about the values and standards that matter to the organization. And as well as being a great example of purpose, it's another great example of flow and harmony between the vision and mission.

FOCUSED

Focus is critical to becoming an Outpacer and it's certainly one of the hardest things to achieve when you are presented with so much opportunity. The mVision can help by guiding your teams on where to focus their energy and resources. It also provides clarity to all of your stakeholders on what you're aiming for.

You want to ensure that the mVision can provide clarity on the customers you're addressing, the markets in which you'll be active and the products or services you'll be delivering. You don't need to cram everything into the mission and vision, as you also have values, strategies and goals. Remember the mVision is a tool, and it's vital that you use all of its components to provide seamless focus to all concerned.

My general rule is that as you deploy teams and individuals, the easiest way to ensure focus is to make sure that what you're asking of them is SMART (specific, measurable, achievable, realistic and timebound). It may seem a little corporate, but if you look at teams and organizations with the highest degree of focus and discipline – the military or sports teams, for example – they all have some version of the SMART approach.

You don't need to be prescriptive to the point of autocratic rule. You're hiring amazing talent and you don't want to stifle them. There should be enough leeway to allow, encourage and enable creativity and freedom, but it needs to be done in a way that ensures your people don't deviate too far. Remember my analogy of the lane sensors in a car.

Finally, you've got to keep it simple. The examples from today's Outpacers are very plain-speaking and easy to understand. Keeping an entire workforce focused is hard enough when you've got a brilliant mVision, so don't fall into the trap of writing corporate verbal garbage that confuses everyone. Test it and test it again. Is it a true representation of what the whole team wants to spend all its energy working towards (because it needs to be!)?

Let's look at an example of a focused mVision:

Amazon:

— Vision: To be Earth's most customer-centric company, where customers can find and discover anything they might want to buy online.

— Mission: We strive to offer our customers the lowest possible prices, the best available selection and the utmost convenience.

Amazon is extremely focused on building scale, and only through this scale can it achieve its mission of low prices. When thinking about entering a new industry, Amazon analyses whether something could be done faster, at a larger scale and with less friction. Industry by industry, starting with books, then moving into toys, clothes, electronics and so on, Amazon is slowly becoming the embodiment of endless selection and frictionless purchasing. This allows it to be loyal to its mVision, offering low prices in every market in which it operates, which it sees as the cornerstone of being a customer-centric company.

COOL

As a father to one teenager (and one catching up fast), I'm aware that if I say something is cool, there's a high chance they will automatically think the opposite! That being said, if you engage your teams in the right way to generate your mVision in the first place, then as a collective group of top talent, you should be able to judge (initially) whether it is cool. Testing the cool factor with your stakeholders should also give you a good indication.

The cool factor is hard to quantify, but it's extremely powerful. Branding experts spend a huge amount of time trying to help brands differentiate by being cool in order to increase their attractiveness and consumer demand. It's hard to argue that isn't important!

It's a word that conveys an attitude, behavior and style that are admired and respected. And by definition, that means it's popular and memorable, which is important because it's got to have appeal to a broad set of stakeholders: talented employees, customers and investors, to name but a few. Being cool doesn't just mean edgy and alternative. It is also something that appeals to the masses and, at its best, reaches iconic status.

Thankfully, you don't need to be a Hollywood A-lister to hit the right note, but you do need to be authentic. Generation Z are a pretty good authority on being cool and when surveyed, 67 per cent said that "being true to their values and beliefs" was what counted. That means being transparent and consistent in all messaging and activity, something that starts with the mVision and permeates through the organization.

So whose values and beliefs matter when creating the mVision? While input from leadership is essential, the answer is everyone in that organization. This is a time when engagement really matters. Whether it's less than ten people as part of a start-up, or a large organization with thousands of people, you've got to know what matters to everyone. If your mVision really doesn't matter to them and it's not part of their values and beliefs, then it will be one of the first things to be pushed aside when they're under pressure. Get to the bottom of what's important to leadership as well as everyone you're counting on to deliver. Stand by it, make it authentic and you have a very good chance of also making it cool.

Let's look at an example of a cool mVision:

Apple:

— Vision: We believe that we are on the face of the earth to make great products and that's not changing. We are here to make the best products on earth, and to leave the world better than we found it.

— Mission: The company is committed to bringing the best user experience to its customers through its innovative hardware, software and services.

You might think that a myopic focus on what customers say they want would be just the recipe for success. But on the contrary, Apple designs products and features that they believe the customer wants before the customer even knows that they want it. Steve Jobs said, "It's really hard to design products by focus groups. A lot of times, people don't know what they want until you show it to them." To me, Apple has a kind of swagger, confidence and authenticity that resonates cool in all they do. The almost universal reaction to a new Apple product is: "That's cool!"

Stay relevant

We've seen how Microsoft changed their mission to include a sense of purpose that resonated with today's stakeholders. Continuously reviewing and, when necessary, refreshing the vision, mission and strategy to ensure the direction of the organization remains inspiring and relevant to customers and stakeholders is a must. The minute your mVision starts to lose relevance, you lose the loyalty of your employees and wider stakeholders, who will start to question what you actually stand for. Here are some examples of how Outpacers have updated their missions:

Facebook:

2012: To give people the power to share and make the world more open and connected.

2020: To give people the power to build community and bring the world closer together.

Amazon:

1995: To be Earth's most customer-centric company, where customers can find and discover anything they might want to buy online, and [which] endeavors to offer its customers the lowest possible prices.

2020: We aim to be Earth's most customer-centric company. Our mission is to continually raise the bar of the customer experience by using the internet and technology to help consumers find, discover and buy anything, and empower businesses and content creators to maximize their success.

Apple:

1980: To make a contribution to the world by making tools for the mind that advance humankind.

2020: To bring the best user experience to its customers through its innovative hardware, software and services.

Netflix:

2002: Our vision is to change the way people access and view the movies they love.

2020: At Netflix, we want to entertain the world.

The old adage that "the only constant is change" is of course true, so don't retreat to the bunker with your head down. If you're communicating well (which means listening, not just talking), you are constantly taking the temperature of key stakeholders and will be assured of your relevance.

Communicate, communicate, communicate

Once you have your vision and mission, you need to ensure that they are communicated clearly and often. Assuming you've done a good job, the mVision will be clear, simple and easy for everyone to understand. You know you're firing on all cylinders when you ask a broad spectrum of individuals internally and externally what the vision and mission are, and they all answer the same. If they don't, try to resist the temptation of blaming everyone else for poor communications. If your mission and vision are as good as they need to be, they should be easy for everyone to grasp, so take another look.

How much communication is needed? A lot! Outpacers treat communication like oxygen for their people: it's always present. We'll dig into this in Chapter 3 on Devoted Talent, but the bottom line is it should be an absolute constant. To this day, Google still holds a weekly session with leadership to communicate key messages and take open questions in a townhall style.

While the Outpacers make it look pretty easy to create an

audacious vision and mission, the reality is that it's actually very hard to create something that motivates employees, customers and key stakeholders. Your vision and mission must transcend the financial to the aspirational. They must be something that all stakeholders see as purposeful and valuable, audacious yet achievable. Outpacers are those that redefine the industry and create groundbreaking value in ways not previously achieved or even dreamt of.

SATYA NADELLA

For me the person who embodies the execution of the Outpacer mVision is Satya Nadella, CEO of Microsoft. There is no doubt that he has had an astonishing impact on Microsoft's indisputable Outpacer status.

When Nadella came to the helm, he instigated a full-scale break from the past. As he would say, he hit "refresh" and successfully reinvented Microsoft. This is all the more remarkable given that he grew up within the business and did not have the outsider perspective of someone less attached but, for him, there were no sacred cows.

Microsoft's original mission of "A computer on every desk and in every home" had (incredibly) been successfully achieved, yet PC sales had slowed, the company was behind in mobile and it needed to grow in gaming. But Nadella's focus went beyond the data from product sales. In his words, Microsoft "needed to build deeper empathy for our customers and their unarticulated and unmet needs".

"Microsoft has always been at its best when it connects personal passion to a broader purpose: Windows, Office, Xbox, Surface, our servers and the Microsoft Cloud – all of these products have become digital platforms upon which individuals and organizations can build their own dreams," he said.

In line with this view, he changed Microsoft's mission statement to: "Our mission is to empower every person and every organization on the planet to achieve more".

Among other hard strategic decisions that would set a new course for the company – including putting Azure rather than Windows at the heart of Microsoft's ambitions – Nadella allowed Office to be available on rival phone operating systems such as iOS. He recognized that collaboration is central to both cloud computing and Microsoft's overall mission, vision and strategy.

Nadella knew that he also had to build a new culture and sense of purpose for an organization that had already achieved one of the most legendary missions ever set out. Empathy would lie at its heart, an approach he credits to the profound effect of his experience as a father of a disabled child.

Nadella's view is that "the C in CEO stands for culture. The CEO is the curator of an organization's culture." I've been fortunate enough to hear Satya's insights on culture and purposeful leadership a few times, and I'm always struck by his incredible authenticity and passion. He perfectly balances the purposeful mission with the capabilities his Microsoft team can bring to people and businesses around the world to allow them "to realize their full potential".

I love it. For me, it ticks every box: it's epic, it's certainly cool, it's focused and it's incredibly purposeful. When you meet people from Microsoft, you can tell it's not just a slogan on the annual report, it's something personal that goes deep into their psyche.

Since being at the helm, Nadella has returned Microsoft to its former glory, becoming the world's biggest company by market cap in 2019 and breaking the $2 trillion market cap point in June 2021.

To be an Outpacer, you need your vision, mission, values and strategy to be aligned to your goals, and then crucially to ensure that the culture supports how it gets done. Nadella may lead a team of around 150,000 people, but he's managed to connect to them on a human level, so they don't just nail what they do, but also how and why they do it.

PHIL JACKSON

I'm a massive admirer of Phil Jackson. For more than twenty years I've been fascinated by his approach to coaching, which, time and again, has been like a magic formula for winning championships. Indeed, he holds the record for the most NBA championships as a player and coach.

When Jackson got his first big NBA coaching role, he was surrounded by a ton of talent, a very clear goal (win a title), a strategy that was working (but not outpacing) and a bunch of people all desperate to make it happen.

In my view the reason Jackson created undeniable Outpacers is that he went beyond the talent, the system and game strategy. He tapped into a higher purpose in his teams that unlocked potential and took them from being great to being some of the best of all time.

Although basketball is a team game, there will always be stars within it whose athleticism, skills and talent outshine anyone else on the court, and for whom fame and wealth follow. They're often well aware of their status. Jackson's coaching staff once took Michael Jordan (the Greatest Of All Time) to one side after a game to chastise him for his lack of team play and tell him, "There's no 'I' in team." His response was, "There may be no 'I' in team, but there's an 'I' in win!" A great story, but reflective of the fact that when you have the talent of a Michael Jordan, a Shaquille O'Neal or a Kobe Bryant, sharing the ball evenly amongst your teammates isn't likely to be the default starting point.

And that was certainly the situation that Jackson found at both the Bulls and the Lakers. Using his influence and leadership skills, he was able to make the would-be hall-of-fame legends listen and convince them to change their ways and play the team game in order to win. Jackson knew that you can have the perfect mix of talent and the best offensive system in the game, you can devise a foolproof defensive strategy and prepare your players for every possible eventuality, but if the players don't have a sense of oneness as a group, your efforts won't pay off.

Why is all this relevant to you? I see a lot of great companies with superb talent, an excellent strategy and happy customers, but they still haven't fulfilled their potential. Sadly, that door to Outpacer greatness will remain closed until they tap into something greater than climbing the corporate ladder or the trappings of corporate success. If there's one-upmanship, dump politics, unhealthy individual competition or individuals only focused on an exit, there's no hope of outpacing. Like Phil Jackson, the CEO has to find a way to have everyone pulling together for something bigger than themselves.

In his pursuit of unity, Jackson explored everything from humanistic psychology to Native American philosophy and even Zen meditation. He was able to develop a new approach to leadership based on freedom, authenticity and selfless teamwork that enabled some of the most talented individual players in history to trust their teammates and work in harmony.

I picked Phil Jackson because he epitomizes what it takes to create and lead an Outpacer. The lesson I'd love you to take is that you can have all the obvious components in place, but without that full commitment to a higher purpose, you can never become an Outpacer

My table for twenty has four guests so far: you, me, Satya Nadella and Phil Jackson. It's already set to be an awesome dinner and it's only going to get better.

CHAPTER 2

ENTREPRENEURIAL CULTURE

In his brilliant book *No Rules Rules*, Netflix co-founder and co-CEO Reed Hastings notes how many of today's businesses continue to operate in ways similar to those founded in the industrial age. He states, "With the growth in importance of intellectual property and creative services, the percentage of the economy that is dependent on nurturing inventiveness and innovation is much higher and continually increasing. Yet most companies are still following the paradigms of the Industrial Revolution." In the industrial age, the goal was to "minimize variation". Successful companies were those that were bigger and better at creating more of the same than their competitors. There was little choice of products, little variation in consumers and little else that could change or disrupt the marketplace.

Things couldn't be more different today. Constant change – not least from globalization, the rate of technological change and consumer behavior – creates uncertainty and opportunity. Today's Outpacers aren't the ones doggedly churning out the same product. Instead, they're the ones grabbing this uncertainty with both hands because of the opportunities it presents. They have an intellectual curiosity and relish the chance to discover new things and steal a march on competitors. They're not trying to pretend change isn't happening. Instead they have a contagious "can do" energy. They're happy to take chances and set new challenges, and have the confidence to do so. All this stems not just from a lone entrepreneur, but from an entrepreneurial culture that drives every move. And as we'll see, it's a culture that defines the organization, regardless of its size.

What does that really mean?

The organization is not beholden to maintaining the status quo. Employees are encouraged to take calculated risks and to do things differently when opportunities present themselves. Everyone in the organization is continuously looking for new opportunities to improve their offering, outpace the competition and grow the business. Customers feel their needs are being predicted and addressed before they know what they are themselves. Failure is considered a necessary consequence of being entrepreneurial and the organization embraces the learnings to become better.

Why is this important?

In today's ultra-competitive global marketplace, organizations must think, invest and act more like a start-up. Entrepreneurial organizations do not wait for new opportunities to emerge; they make their own opportunities. They ruthlessly pursue growth. They thrive on competition and are willing to take chances to make big gains. An Outpacer is able to combine entrepreneurial culture with sound processes and deep experience to develop and win in new markets.

Compared to the mVision characteristic, entrepreneurial culture is a little less tangible, and harder to create and sustain, but its benefits are incredible. The analogy of a flywheel is often overused, but in this case it fits. Once entrepreneurial culture is in motion, the momentum continues to build of its own volition and catapults everything forward at an amazing velocity.

Let's be clear that there is a difference between being an entrepreneur and having an entrepreneurial culture. I've worked for and with some great entrepreneurs during my time in industry and I've also acted as an advisor to many more. It's fair to say true entrepreneurs are a very rare phenomenon.

Compare it to sport, where many of us play our chosen sport with great passion and dedication, but very few make it to the pros. When you meet or see a professional athlete in the sport you play, you quickly realize that they are made of different stuff. The same is true with real standout entrepreneurs. When you meet one, they just seem to be wired differently.

Importantly, and thankfully, I don't believe that to create an Outpacer you need to be a bona fide entrepreneur. I also don't believe that trying to hire a bunch of entrepreneurs is the way to go (real entrepreneurs want to work for themselves anyway). What is important is that you bottle the benefits of being entrepreneurial, scale them and make them part of the fabric of your organization so that you can outpace the competition. There is no doubt in my mind that it's an imperative to being an Outpacer.

While for me, being an entrepreneur is a pretty straightforward thing (you either are or you aren't!), an entrepreneurial culture is something that can either be preserved (from the founders' original starting point) or, if not there today, it can be nurtured and developed.

Look at Sir Richard Branson. There's no doubting his entrepreneur credentials. It's true that Virgin and Branson are pretty interchangeable terms – it's hard to imagine one without the other, and it would seem that it's Sir Richard's unbelievable force of character that drives everything. But there are over 400 businesses that have carried the Virgin name, and Sir Richard, even with his unassailable enthusiasm, has not personally overseen the development of each. Instead, he has fostered a culture that resonates throughout every organization. Unlike other Outpacers, the Virgin Group isn't united by a technical insight or a remarkable piece of innovation. It's their entrepreneurial culture that is the unifying factor.

I would argue that you don't need an entrepreneur running a business today for it to have an entrepreneurial culture. Google, Microsoft and Amazon are not run by entrepreneurs (rather those that have excelled and come up through the business), but they certainly have an entrepreneurial culture and reap the benefits of it on a daily basis. In fact, to be an Outpacer, a business's entrepreneurial spirit can't be driven by just one person. It must become pervasive across the organization – it has to become part of the culture.

For me, the best definition of culture is "the way things get done around here". In an Outpacer, that tends to be pretty amazing! Most of the organizations we profiled in the first chapter are famous for their cultures. Large traditional corporates tour Silicon Valley every few years and marvel at the culture created by many there. They want to learn and bring back some of that magic dust to their own organization. The challenge is that, despite the best intentions, an entrepreneurial culture can't be created simply by placing table tennis or foosball tables around the office. To be successful, the culture needs to be authentic and not a standalone thing.

How do you know if you've got that culture? There are six key elements that you should be able to point to within your organization, demonstrating that you have what it takes to outpace. (But if you're asking the question in the first place, you probably won't find them!)

There's no picking and choosing. All six need to be in place for an entrepreneurial culture to take hold and flourish.

Contagious energy

Becoming an Outpacer is very, very hard. To reach that level of success is an incredible feat and not something that happens overnight. It follows a relentless push to succeed. It may look easy from the outside, but it requires commitment. The same is true whatever the field of endeavor. Stage performers who look completely natural will have meticulously organized every inch of the performance. Sports stars will put in hours and hours of practice – 10,000 of them being "the magic number of greatness", if Malcolm Gladwell's views in *Outliers* are to be believed.

To continue working at that level requires an almost endless source of energy – an energy that is contagious and bounces off one person to the next. Think of a first-time marathon runner, who hits the wall at 19 miles and can't imagine how they'll continue. It's the group of runners around them that gives them the energy to get through it and complete the race when, running on their own, they would have gone home thinking 19 miles is good enough. When you have that sort of contagious energy, you don't have to worry about how hard people are working or if they're putting in the hours. You can be sure that everyone is motivated and motivating each other to achieve the mission.

This energy supercharges the creativity and problem solving that are essential to outpacing the competition.

Feeding into contagious energy is a strong sense of purpose. An organization will find more energy if it knows why it's doing something, and it has total belief in it.

Look twice

Outpacers will challenge everything. The prevailing attitude is that nothing is ever finished, and everything can be improved. For some, this can be too exhausting to be around. They would much rather follow a clear set of rules, complete their specific tasks without being challenged too much and know they've done a good job. These individuals have a great deal to contribute – but not at an Outpacer.

If you're looking twice, you're not stuck in the weeds, worrying about the detail without thinking about the bigger picture. You are able to stand back from the strategy, thinking about the vision and mission, looking to see if the current course is actually correct.

One CEO I worked for was giving high praise to one of our colleagues on their flawless execution, until they added for me to keep a close eye on them because "they'll project manage themselves off a cliff!" It stuck with me because it was so true. This individual was totally dedicated to their project plan, but wasn't allowing enough time to check in and ensure that delivering that plan was still the right thing to do. An entrepreneurial culture requires everyone to look twice at what they're doing, to make sure it's the optimal way of doing it and that delivering it is aligned to the mVision.

Love

In an entrepreneurial culture it's personal. It's not just a job, it means so much more, sometimes everything. That phrase "it's personal" is very powerful, and in my experience it means someone is about to do everything in their power. Much like contagious energy, in an Outpacer a love for what you do is shared with those around you and brings with it a commitment, almost an obsession to get to that destination. Just think about the power of a group of individuals all feeling that same way. That's not to say it will be plain sailing. As with any loving relationship, there will be ups and downs. The road to becoming an Outpacer is often anything but smooth.

Smash through the muscle memory

My trainer talks about muscle memory being key to new athletic breakthroughs. Once your brain says, "OK, I know I can do this", you can really progress. But the key thing is to break that part of the brain that says it hurts too much and can't be done. Outpacers smash through the muscle memory by pushing the boundaries and limits that others set (it's the audacious part of the mVision), creating the environment for breathtaking innovation.

By smashing through the muscle memory, you take the shackles off the organization, fostering innovation and setting higher standards that were previously believed to be impossible. For Outpacers, the greater the challenge, the greater the satisfaction. As Sir Richard Branson puts it, "My interest in life comes from setting myself huge, apparently unachievable challenges and trying to rise above them."

No fear

Having no fear is a common trait among entrepreneurs. It stems from their total belief in their mVision and their ability, which makes them often oblivious to other perspectives or sometimes even facts!

Often, the questions they'll pose are: what's there to be scared of? What's the worst that could happen? In an entrepreneurial culture, that lack of fear translates into a belief that failure is a risk worth taking, and everyone is on board.

By contrast, in traditional corporates, the things that many hold dear (reputation, wealth, stability, promotion) are the same things that create the fear and stop people from doing something entrepreneurial.

An Outpacer risk function has the job of maximizing the risk the organization can take. The risk function in a non-Outpacer sets out to minimize the risk taken. You see the difference. There is of course a balance to be struck. Taking risks doesn't mean anything goes. We'll explore more of this in Chapter 8 on Enabling Governance because getting that balance right is a critical element of a thriving entrepreneurial culture.

Know who's boss

One of the attractions of being an entrepreneur is to become your own boss, but the world's most successful entrepreneurs know that the real boss is the customer. Their focus will be on solving a problem for the customer – whether they know they have a problem or not.

Virgin Records was born out of the mail-order business that Sir Richard started running in his student magazine. In his words, "Virgin's first record shop had to incorporate all [the] aspects of how music fitted into people's lives. In exploring how to do this, I think we created the conceptual framework of what Virgin later became." That framework was centered around customer enjoyment: "We wanted the Virgin Records shop to be an enjoyable place to go at a time when record buyers were given short shrift. We wanted to relate to the customer, not patronize them." Customers had been able to buy records before, so they didn't know that they had a problem, but the Virgin experience opened their eyes to how much better things could be when you could hang out in the shop with your friends, listening to your favorite records like you were sitting in your front living room!

Not content with the small retailing margins that the shop brought home, Branson decided to see if the focus on the customer could be applied to other parts of the music industry. He seized on the recording industry, as he had "heard that conditions [in recording studios] were extremely formal . . . bands would often have to record straight after breakfast. The idea of the Rolling Stones having to record 'Brown Sugar' straight after finishing their bowls of cornflakes struck me as ridiculous." So Virgin would do it differently.

Their vision was that "the best environment for making records would be a big, comfortable house in the country where a band could come and stay for weeks at a time and record whenever they felt like it, probably in the evening". To buy "The Manor", an old country house near Oxford, Virgin had to gather all the money they could. To take that bold decision shows their confidence in that insight. The Manor could be rented out by bands that enjoyed the flexibility and comfort.

Virgin Records had twenty years of success, culminating in 1992, when Thorn EMI bought it for $1 billion. The company's life charts the progression of the kind of entrepreneurial culture for which Virgin would become famous – finding new opportunities to serve the customer above all else and better than anyone else.

These six factors combined are the cornerstones to an entrepreneurial culture. That culture can deliver a huge amount to an organization, ensuring that it makes its own opportunities, ruthlessly pursues growth, takes risks, thrives on competition and does whatever it takes to delight the boss. That culture doesn't come about by chance. It requires a shift in mindset, attitude and approach, as shown below.

How to do it:

Move from:	**Move to:**
Short-term outlook	Long-term outlook
Rules	Trust
Fear	Confidence
Risk aversion	Maximizing risk
Shared accountability	Clear ownership
Returning cash to investors	Reinvesting
Achievable goals	Big Hairy Audacious Goals/ Moonshot (see p. 50)
Closed to new ways	Exploring
Focus on investors	Focus on customers

Long-term outlook

Outpacers do an excellent job of having a long-term outlook instead of a short-term view. Many businesses find themselves forced into a quarterly cycle that's driven by investors, but that ultimately leads to the whole business being too focused on the short term. The average CEO tenure is less than five years, and there is often a fear of being fired within that window. The natural inclination is to hunker down and focus on the immediate rather than seeing the bigger picture potential and the business's role in the broader economy and society.

An Outpacer will have set a long-term vision for doing something that seems completely incredible. If you can start to paint a picture of something that sounds incredible, you will motivate people who want to be taken on what sounds like the most fantastic ride. It may well take a long time, but it will be worthwhile. That sort of vision will inspire the talent within the business and turn a job into a journey.

Think of Google's mission to organize the world's information. Twenty years ago, they first started to plan digitizing a whole library. At the time that sounded crazy to many, but what it did achieve was to get a bunch of talented engineers very excited.

Trust

They may not thank you for it but think of great talent as a group of teenagers. They need their freedom. You can only put rules around them for so long; at a certain point you have to trust that when they are out, they are doing the right thing. If you set too many hard and fast rules around talent, they will never push the boundaries or go past those rules. And while the rules might have worked when they were first implemented, in traditional corporates they end up staying there past their sell-by date and become accepted as "the way things are".

To establish and maintain an entrepreneurial culture, you have to trust your people to make the (right) decisions. Netflix famously allows its employees to take as much holiday as they want. Other Outpacers have followed suit, including LinkedIn, who recognize the perfect alignment between the policy (or non-policy) and one of their stated values, to "act like an owner". Intelligent people should be trusted to make good decisions. Don't throw the rule book out of the window, but allow some freedom, which will empower talented staff looking to spread their wings a little. As Reed Hastings says: "Don't provide a musical score and build a symphonic orchestra. Work on creating those jazz conditions and hire the type of employees who long to be part of an improvisational band."

On the flip side, what does lack of trust look like? Like talking to someone in a call center to get a problem resolved that doesn't fit within the company's processes. The polite but exasperated response is: "I hear what you are saying, and it makes perfect sense, but I'm not allowed to do that." That is a traditional corporate nightmare, and you'll never hear it at an Outpacer.

Confidence

Confidence exists at both a personal and a cultural level. At an Outpacer, you'll find both, with one feeding off the other. It works like a sports team where each individual has belief but together there is strength in numbers. If one person starts to feel uneasy, the others step up to help, making the team stronger. You hire great people who are confident in their abilities. Put enough of them together and put your trust in them, and it starts to build an organizational confidence. People feel emboldened to make decisions in line with the mVision that other organizations would hesitate to take.

The confidence needs to come from the top and be demonstrable. Making decisions swiftly is a prime example. Imagine a company deciding whether or not to launch a new product. A quick decision creates confidence that leadership are supportive of the team behind the product, and that it's a good idea to go to market. If leadership prevaricates, puts a committee together and takes a month to consider it, confidence is replaced with concern. How can it take that long? What are they worried about?

Not every decision made will be right, but making a decision is better than not making one, which erodes confidence. If it proves to be the wrong decision, leadership should take the ultimate responsibility and move on. Leaders within Outpacers explain why the decision was taken in the first place and are able to articulate what went wrong, how the organization has learnt from it and why it won't happen again, before concluding by saying, "Let's go, next product please" – and all without trying to find a fall guy or girl. The message sent out is that the organization is not stopping just because it failed. Instead, it is more confident even as a result of the failure, because knowledge has been increased by understanding what went wrong. Big tech talks about fast failure. If you're going to fail, do it fast, shut it down, learn from it and move on.

Maximizing risk

Obviously, no company is looking to fail. I once had a boss who said to me, "Failure is completely fine, as long as you don't make a habit out of it!" In traditional corporates, there are many people who are simply looking to pay their bills, and if there's a chance that their job security could be impacted by trying to do something risky, they won't. There's no impetus to reach for the stars. The negative consequences of failure seem greater than the upsides of success. If you have a group of people who are all thinking that way, it's very difficult to break that cultural mold.

Instilling a culture of maximizing risk is not as simple as leadership saying, "It's OK, there's no consequence for you failing here." People have to be given the right tools and the right environment, otherwise they are being set up to fail. First and foremost, it comes down to a good governance model that allows you to calculate your level of risk. I'll cover this in more detail in Chapter 8.

Transparency is also key: being able to see that any risks that are taken are manageable within the portfolio. Financial commitments still have to be met and budgets have to be hit. Any risks that are taken need to be balanced across the product portfolio. Some people look at the activity of businesses with an entrepreneurial culture like Tesla or Virgin and think some of the decisions are reckless. That's far from true. Each decision is a calculated risk on balance to allow them to achieve their financial commitments but still find opportunities to massively pursue growth.

To outpace you also need open communication and flat structures. In a hierarchical environment, it's hard for the product manager to build up enough rapport with the boss to allow open and collaborative conversation. A once-a-month meeting won't cut it. A flatter structure, where people talk freely and openly, allows for brainstorming and greater innovation.

Clear ownership

If, in an organization, there are a large number of people responsible for a program, or multiple accountabilities for a product launch, that shared accountability often means that no one is ultimately on the hook for it. If something goes wrong, people will roll their shoulders and say it wasn't their fault, pointing out all the other people who were involved.

Outpacers don't like having a group of people responsible for something. You rarely make great decisions by committee, and it can definitely become a case of too many cooks spoiling the broth. It's also demotivating, whereas, with the right characters, the opposite is true of real accountability. People working at Outpacers don't run away from responsibility, but towards it. They want to know that their actions have directly contributed to the outcome, good or bad. They are given the responsibility and ownership that they have yearned for forever. It's a motivating factor to be responsible and clearly accountable for something. All those individuals are focused on a successful outcome. For some that's like walking on stage and having to speak in public – it's the stuff of nightmares – but for someone with an

Outpacer mentality it's motivating rather than debilitating. It's that level of confidence and desire to have their moment in the spotlight.

You don't need to have an organization full of people looking for greater exposure to be an Outpacer. You just need them in the right roles. A football team ('soccer' for my American friends) needs strikers to keep on shooting and believing that the next shot will land in the back of the net. The players in defense have an equally valid role in the team, are equally talented, and also fully supportive of the striker's efforts. To succeed everyone needs to play in position.

Don't make the mistake of thinking that shining the spotlight and assigning responsibility in this way will lead to a blame culture. A blame culture is only created if people *blame* the people that are responsible. This comes back to my point about leadership. Rather than publicly shaming the person who was accountable, an outpacing leader will explain why that product went wrong, what was learnt and how the next product or idea taken up by that individual will have leadership's complete backing.

Reinvesting

It might seem odd to talk about investment in a chapter on entrepreneurial culture, but without funding, you can't move forward even if you have the best culture in the world. Amazon is known for its philosophy of taking its profits and reinvesting them, rather than offering large dividends to incentivize investors to reinvest. It understands the business's dependence on investors, but equally has always wanted investors to understand that greater benefits will come down the line from a company growing and expanding by innovating. Deciding where the trade-off is between keeping investors happy and growing the business is a balancing act and requires confident decision-making at board level. If you're confident in your reinvestment strategy but your investors don't agree, you'll need to decide whether it's a misunderstanding that can be talked through, or a more terminal misalignment.

Big, hairy, audacious goals

One of my favorite business books is *Built to Last* by Jim Collins. In it, Collins talks about BHAGs or Big Hairy Audacious Goals, the beauty of the term being that it needs no explanation. Google's parent company Alphabet has its own form of BHAGs, which they call moonshots. Some take on seismic proportions. One of its biggest moonshots is Waymo, the organization's multi-billion dollar investment in autonomous cars. Not all these moonshots succeed. Google Glass was an incredible development in smart glasses, but due to privacy concerns and what some perceived as a clunky design, it didn't take off from a consumer perspective at that time. What links each moonshot is how audacious the goal is, how much it defies the odds and how spectacular it will be if it succeeds.

If you set the goal too low, you will never know how far you could go. I mentioned muscle memory earlier. The way to enable people to go beyond the limit that they have set themselves is to tell them to go further than they think they can. Set achievable goals and everyone will be satisfied when they are reached. Set audacious goals and everyone will be in awe, inspired and prepared to put in more effort than they knew they were capable of.

Exploring

Outpacers possess intellectual curiosity. They will take something that has been done a certain way for a long time and worked perfectly well, and ask whether there is a way it could be done better. There's none of the fear of change that holds many people back, but rather a cultural openness. If someone suggests something new, everyone will at least give it airtime to consider if it is a better way.

It may be that appetite to explore is not immediately obvious as it's being quashed by others in the organization, often middle managers who wrongly see any form of change as a threat. In that environment, it's up to leadership to play a role. I once dealt with a company that was struggling with high costs. Despite repeated requests, managers weren't doing enough to bring them down. The leadership team's next move was to say that anyone in the organization who can find a way to bring costs down will personally receive 10 per cent of the savings generated by their idea in the first year. Middle managers were the fat who were hindering progress. By circumnavigating them, the leadership encouraged the rest of the organization to speak out in a culture where they had felt suppressed. The middle managers saw the writing on the wall from that moment on – either you get with the program or there's no place for you.

Focus on customers

As we've established, the customer is the boss, and deserving of your obsessive attention. One of the most important times to demonstrate this is when reporting results. I am not diminishing the significance of the financial element of quarterly reporting, it's obviously very important for the session to go well. But if you set the quarterly results as *the* financial focus, then you can send the wrong message to your people – both employees and external stakeholders – that the customer plays second fiddle. Make the customer prominent in your results over everything else. Talk about customer satisfaction, loyalty, churn, customer acquisition and the lifetime value of a customer. Obsess about the customer, have your investors obsess about the customer and the message will get through to the organization. But if the financial results are an overwhelming spreadsheet of complex financial reporting, then the message sent back is that the numbers trump the customer. If you set the right metrics and targets around the customer, reporting great earnings to your investors will follow.

How to keep the entrepreneurial culture alive

I'll conclude this chapter with something of a reality check. In the words of Marshall Goldsmith, "what got you here won't get you there". Not everyone is capable of, or even wants to make the adjustment from being part of a start-up to a big organization. The people who started the company may not be the ones who help you scale the company. It's definitely not true that because you were there at the start, that means you can't continue on the journey. Facebook and Amazon are great examples of companies that scaled with their founders, but it doesn't work for everyone. It's a question of desire rather than capability. People must be willing to adapt the skills they brought to the original business and flex that into a large-scale business.

Once you have created a product or service, scaling up requires continual development. The people involved from the outset may just get bored of countless iterations of the same product and want to do something entirely different. There will also be people who are not capable of operating in a bigger, more scaled business. As the organization grows, some sort of enabling governance will be essential. There will need to be some structure; it's not realistic to think that people will wander into the founder's office and scratch heads around the white board for a couple of hours. Some might miss having that access and resent the feeling that they are a small cog in a big wheel. A more structured environment may be anathema to the adrenaline junkies who thrive on living on the edge, not knowing if they will get paid, but relishing the risk inherent in the knowledge that if one person fails, the whole setup could be brought down.

That is totally fine. It would be romantic idealism to think that everyone who started in a small business has the capability and/or desire to stay with it. If they want to leave, it's something to watch for but not necessarily something to be sad about. Don't go out of your way to try to hang on to those people out of a kind of sentimental loyalty. Hang on to those who have the desire and capability to go on the journey you're committed to with your mVision.

As you are growing and evolving, so too must your culture change to match your stage of growth. It doesn't mean that you're not innovative any more, but the way that you go about innovation will have to be different. You'll have to ask for funding, for example, which will mean dealing with external investors who will have a say over how things are run. The most important thing is to stay true to the mVision. What is the organization trying to do?

You have the opportunity to grow an incredible business, but you can't do it if you're not in tune with what will help you scale. Think of great musicians who started out making incredible music but succumbed to the dark side of the music (and fame) industry, and didn't have the discipline to go on to have long and illustrious careers. You don't want to be the cautionary tale of amazing potential that was never fulfilled. Look at the Rolling Stones. Adding a certain level of professionalism hasn't diminished their creative talent – or their ability to enjoy the ride!

ELON MUSK

Elon Musk is undoubtedly an entrepreneur, but for me he goes beyond that. He has the seldom witnessed ability to share his gift with others, repeat his entrepreneurial feats time and time again at massive scale and take thousands of colleagues and customers on the journey of a lifetime. He creates an entrepreneurial culture across all that he does.

Musk is widely admired and has a cult-like following. But don't make the mistake of thinking it's all about him. I believe he is a genius, but even he can't possibly achieve all that he has without an incredible team of devoted talent around him. His gift is not only being an entrepreneur, but having the ability to share and disseminate that gift broadly – scaling the "Musk effect".

Musk was accepted into Stanford, but true to form was only able to contain his energy and desire to start a business for two days! No joke, he left to launch his first company, Zip2 Corporation, with his brother in 1995, which he successfully sold to Compaq for ~$300 million.

Perhaps this early success was rocket fuel (pun intended) to an individual who showed no fear in taking on some colossal challenges: an internet bank, an electric car company, a space company and even a company focused on developing brain–machine interfaces. These ventures took courage to start and even more to see them through to a position where they have been successful. Both SpaceX and Tesla ran into extreme difficulty a few years in, but with Musk's no-fear attitude they've both gone on to incredible success.

Musk may be impulsive, but his investments and ventures are diligently researched before he jumps in. Tesla and SpaceX are both active in industries that had not been known for being disrupted. The scale of innovation that SpaceX has brought to the space exploration industry, and that Tesla has brought to the electrification of cars, is hard to overstate.

There's no doubt working in a Musk company isn't for everyone – but neither is being entrepreneurial. Musk says, "I think it is possible for ordinary people to choose to be extraordinary." And that's kind of the point. He takes "ordinary" bright people who want to be great and inspires them to achieve things as a collective that they couldn't have done without him. For me that's an entrepreneurial culture because his belief helps carry the collective.

That ceaseless ambition from the top is infectious throughout the company, as Josh Boehm, a former SpaceX worker, explains: "The thing is no one, especially not Elon, is forcing you to work long hours. SpaceX just hires self-driven people who are extremely passionate about the mission. Long hours is just usually what it takes to get the job done."

Musk also encourages his employees to look twice, instructing them, "In general, always pick common sense as your guide. If following a 'company rule' is obviously ridiculous in a particular situation, such that it would make for a great Dilbert cartoon, then the rule should change."

He clearly loves what he does and, despite the seriousness of the incredible challenges he takes on, he still has fun with it. Not many would think about allowing owners to put their car into dance mode so it blares out music by Trans-Siberian Orchestra and puts on a light show!

I'm a big fan of his straight-talking approach, his less than conventional style and his unencumbered ambition. More than that, he and his teams create Outpacers that have an entrepreneurial culture and change the world.

REESE WITHERSPOON

She may historically be better known for her on-screen Oscar-winning performances, but Reese Witherspoon is quickly and rightly becoming recognized as a very successful entrepreneur. She is a book club founder, Draper James clothing line owner and, more recently, the successful seller of her production company Hello Sunshine to venture capital for almost $1 billion in 2021, a deal that marks her as one of the most powerful players in the entertainment industry. And what's more, she's driving incredible and important change in Tinsel Town.

I'm picking someone from outside the traditional corporate environment as I believe we can learn from successful people in any walk of life. Outpacers share a desire, even demand, for insights and lessons from every possible source. They have intellectual curiosity and a need for diverse input, which creates a breadth of insight that helps them see things others have missed. It allows them to "look twice" better than most.

Witherspoon may have had limited business experience but, as she saw it, she certainly wasn't light on experience. She treated venture capital pitches like auditions and drew on her skills of teamwork, communications and inclusion of team members. And that's a great lesson to take away. You may not possess everything you need for a new journey, but you're most certainly equipped, so be like Reese, focus on what you do have and make the most of it.

To create an entrepreneurial culture, I look for someone who has the ability to take their unique skills and talents, scale them with a broader team and replicate them time and time again. Every new TV series or movie can be considered a standalone business – with separate funding requirements and the right teams to run each "business" successfully. Much like a retail chain, if a few episodes (stores) start underperforming, they can bring the whole thing down. The number of hits that Witherspoon has produced is all the more impressive then, especially considering she is also pursuing a purpose that drives her to right many of the well-known wrongs done to women in Hollywood.

Witherspoon matches business acumen with a feminist commitment to women's stories, as seen in her wildly successful streaming hits. *Big Little Lies*, *The Morning Show* and *Little Fires Everywhere* all combined female-led casts with hot-button social themes. In addition to employing large numbers of women via her Hello Sunshine projects, Witherspoon, a founding and vocal member of the Time's Up movement, has taken on issues such as pay parity, persuading HBO to reshape its entire policy to retroactively ensure pay parity on its shows. Her ability to smash through the muscle memory or, in other words, smash the glass ceiling for women is hugely impressive.

Described in 2021 as "Hollywood's richest female actor", there's no doubt that she can add the title of Outpacer to her numerous accolades. Given her "contagious energy" (Meryl Streep once likened her to a hummingbird) and well-known love of tequila shots, she'll also be a welcome addition to our dinner party! There's so much inspiration to take from what she's done already and what she will do in the future.

I have no idea what it's like to be a woman in business, but I do know that I am privileged and that being a white man has unfairly contributed to my success. I champion those who fight against injustice and bias. I'm sure Witherspoon has inspired and will continue to inspire many women, but she's also inspired me in the fight that she has taken on, and she has become an archetype for creating an entrepreneurial culture within the Outpacers that she has created.

So, to little girls everywhere, "when people try to tell you to stay in your lane, don't listen. Do not listen."

CHAPTER 3

DEVOTED TALENT

What does that really mean?

Put simply, the talent is the best of the best and they love what they do. They are engaged, collaborating and determined to achieve a common and well-articulated mVision. Often they feel that the company's mVision is purposeful and that they can make a positive impact on society at large. Every person understands how to contribute to the organization's success; they are enabled and motivated with stretching and aligned goals. Diversity in all senses is a must and employees are expected to contribute and collaborate, regardless of title, grade or experience. The organization sets clear career paths and creates opportunities for employees to develop and excel. It offers a great rewards package where everyone shares in the financial benefits of success. Everyone is devoted to achieving the mVision.

Why is this important?

Being devoted has traditionally been more closely associated with areas outside of the corporate environment: a personal relationship, a sports team, an environmental mission, a social or political movement. But it's a key part of the DNA of an Outpacer.

When people are devoted to a purposeful endeavor, they are more engaged in driving towards success and will go the extra mile to achieve it. Talent turnover is often lower and the percentage of high performers is usually higher at organizations where the workforce is more engaged. Engaged and devoted employees are more willing to identify and learn new skills and capabilities that eventually lead to increased productivity and competitive advantages, which are key to becoming an Outpacer.

People often suggest that you should be able to answer whether you live to work, or work to live. The question is fully loaded and is rarely a topic of conversation in an Outpacer, but it is one I remember discussing with a group of mates. I was in a role that I loved. When I wasn't at work, I was thinking about it, trying to figure out every conceivable way to outperform.

My job was in an industry that fascinated me, I was working with people who shared my values, I got to meet great people every day, I travelled and I had experiences that I couldn't have had without my job. I was challenged, learning and getting rewarded, leading to further opportunity for my family to do great things. I loved it. In short, I was devoted to my job.

As I looked around me and listened, it was clear nobody else felt like me. Unfortunately, some didn't even like their jobs, let alone love them. I felt – and still feel – very fortunate to be in a situation where work has enriched my life. Outpacers are similarly driven by a group of people who are motivated, compelled to achieve a goal, working hard and enjoying it. They're in love with their work. They are devoted.

Devoted may seem an unusual word to describe something associated with work. You may associate it with a loved one, or hear it used by an artist or religious leader. But for those who feel a personal connection with work, describe what they do as a purposeful endeavor and know that it brings out their best, devotion feels appropriate. Put a large group of people together who all feel the same way, and it's very powerful.

I'm not advocating for a bunch of workaholics. Everyone must have an escape from work, and spending time with family and friends, hanging out and following pursuits away from the office are really important. But equally, I'm keen to dispel the idea that you can't get a great deal of happiness and fulfillment from your job.

People often talk about a work–life balance – I think of it as a work–life blend – and the importance of aligning an individual's passion with their work environment. Health and happiness rely on there being no mismatch between the two. We spend a lot of time at work. Whether you enjoy it or not it is often a deciding factor in your overall mental health and wellbeing.

In my view, being devoted is the best possible way to describe how you want the people in any organization to feel about their work. You want them to love what they do. Confucius probably said it best: "Choose a job you love, and you will never have to work a day in your life." That's so true. An Outpacer should be full of people not working a day in their life!

Nirvana or reality?

If you're reading this slightly cynically, thinking that I'm describing nirvana rather than reality, then I have a small amount of sympathy with your view. I agree, you're unlikely to create a workforce made up of completely devoted people, and even the most devoted people wake up some days and just want to pull their duvet over their heads!

But you should have gathered by now that only by aiming for the moon will you ever get there! So don't be what I call the "anomaly hunter", taking the negative view and trying to find holes in everything. See the bigger picture and focus on building a devoted team. And don't forget you can always ask anyone who doesn't match up to leave. Look at the Netflix approach to those not meeting expectations: "Adequate performance gets a generous severance package."

The road to devotion

There are a number of key elements that you need to have in place to ensure you have devoted talent. They are all interconnected and of equal importance – you can't afford to drop the ball on any.

Ultimately, with great talent, it all comes down to creating the right chemistry. It's a match-making process, aligning the mVision to each individual in the organization and then sustaining it through the entrepreneurial culture that you are carefully nurturing. If you're starting from scratch, you get the chance to do that rigorously from the very beginning of the organization's journey. If you're already established and needing to "course-correct", it's about working out who is or can be devoted, and who can't. Those that can't need to be shown the door, fast.

Here are the eight elements for devoted talent.

SELECTION

There's plenty of devoted talent to be found outside of corporate life, even in places where financial reward is appalling and risk of death is high. If you can find devoted talent in these kind of situations, it can't be that hard where the financial reward is high and the chance of death is almost zero!

Let's look at the military, specifically at the British Special Forces unit, the Special Air Service (SAS), whose motto is "who dares wins". It was the first Special Forces unit in the world and, given that I'm British, I will argue (with total bias) that it's the best of the best and an example of devoted talent.

SAS selection is reputed to be among the toughest in the world, with an average pass rate of 10 per cent that dipped as low as 3–4 per cent in the 1990s. The SAS selection program is so grueling and rigorous that in some years no candidates have managed to pass.

I'm not suggesting that to create an Outpacer you need to immediately issue an instruction to HR suggesting that all candidates be sent on grueling marches, assessed for combat survival and put through horrendous interrogation! But I am saying that we can learn from the pride the SAS take in such a tough selection process and the discipline with which candidates – even good candidates – are rejected.

I first witnessed this type of ruthless selection in the business world at Energis, where turnaround legend Archie Norman had been brought in to chair the organization and find the right people to rapidly change its trajectory (which is exactly what happened, doubling the value of the business to $1 billion in just four years).

The person he put in charge of this talent treasure hunt was Roger Philby. Philby loves to tell the story of how, after spending a considerable amount of the company's money to run an assessment center for external candidates, he was asked by the chairman to report back on progress to a gathering of the extended leadership team. Norman asked Philby to let the group know just how many people he'd hired after spending so much on the assessment center. Philby started looking slightly flushed, and with good reason, given that the answer he was forced to announce to the entire room was zero! He was understandably worried he was about to be thrown under the bus.

But Norman didn't see it that way. He started clapping and told the leadership team, "Roger kept a bunch of people who would not have succeeded at Energis from our door. I'd say that's a good day at work. Congratulations."

Saying no is important, but how do you find those most likely to be devoted talent? The answer lies in the personality of the individual. Rather than probing *what* they've done, find out *why* they did it. When thinking about what that should sound like, make sure you know why you're doing what you do. If you're surrounded by devoted talent, make sure you've profiled why they do what they do as well. That insight is gold dust to an Outpacer.

Once you're meeting potential candidates, don't just focus on their CV. Think about what other indicators of talent and devotion they have in their lives. Perhaps it's a hobby or not-for-profit. How do they measure up when discussing that, and how passionate are they about it? Evidence of past performance is the best indicator of future performance.

One of my favorite questions to ask in an interview is: "What motivates you?" Some will give you the answers they think you want to hear, but you can always tell the ones that are authentic. One of the things that I try to find out is whether this individual even knows themselves. If they're driven and motivated (and likely to become devoted), usually that person is aware of that driving force within. It's a personal and emotional thing, but it's seldom hard to find if you know how to look for it.

It all starts with selection. Get that right and you're on your way.

DIVERSITY

Diversity, in all senses of the word, is crucial to devoted talent. While diversity and inclusion have been a topic of focus for years, it seems that the start of this decade is finally seeing recognition of Diversity, Equity and Inclusion (DE&I) as more than a PR agenda item. KPMG's 2021 CEO Survey revealed that more than 60 per cent of CEOs had Social as their number one priority on their ESG agenda.

The danger of "group think" from a non-diverse team is very real. A diverse team brings diversity of thought, absolutely crucial to the Outpacer. Excelling at DE&I has the double benefit of increasing competitiveness and also increasing the pool of devoted talent.

The topic of DE&I is difficult for many, and not for many good reasons. While there are a host of great reasons to have a diverse team from a competitive standpoint, the most important reason is that it's undoubtedly the right thing to do. So while I could go on for pages about the undoubted advantages of having a diverse team, I'm not going to. Instead I'm going to focus on how you do it. (If you need to learn more about why, feel free to put this book down, take a deep breath and realize you're exactly the kind of person who will never be an Outpacer.)

Stephen Frost, who led the DE&I Team for the 2012 London Olympics, knows a thing or two about both diversity and devoted talent. His advice for successful incorporation of DE&I is "understand, lead and deliver". Understand what you are trying to do and why, and work back from there. Understand that not only is it the right thing to do, but it is also mission critical to have diversity of thought and input. There are plenty of examples of this mission criticality. Think of the voice recognition systems that failed to accurately recognize women's voices as they had been programd by men. Or soap dispensers that wouldn't dispense soap to a Black hand as the optic sensors failed to register the skin tone.

The world is not perfect, and while you, as you're still reading, understand the importance of DE&I, there may be others within the organization who are less aware. Stephen talks of intrinsic and extrinsic motivators. If people are not intrinsically motivated towards DE&I by their own experiences and beliefs, extrinsic motivators such as targets can be effective. Targets, as opposed to quotas, can be dynamic and move with the organization as it grows. By setting targets, leadership demonstrates that this is a priority, as what gets measured matters. Not only should this help deliver the end result, but also people who are set targets are obliged to do research and carve out some mental time for further thought, or perhaps have conversations with someone they otherwise wouldn't have. That may arouse the intellectual curiosity that exists in a real Outpacer and bring greater understanding across the board. Even Outpacers who are at the top of their game can benefit from targets – it would be hubris to think otherwise.

ENVIRONMENT

There is an undeniable link between culture and environment. It's impossible to have one without the other.

I love the quote from W. Clement Stone: "You are a product of your environment. So choose the environment that will best develop you toward your objective." Devoted talent is like a heat-seeking missile when it comes to finding a great environment in which to work.

While environment and culture are interlinked (with environment feeding into culture), there is a difference. The environment is made up of the *surroundings* and *influences* on your people. They are two levers that can be pulled and will have a distinct impact on the output of an organization, which in turn plays its part in developing the culture. Culture (in my definition) is the way that people do things around here. It's a subtle difference, but important to recognize. If you can regulate and nurture the environment, you will feed the culture that can catapult everything forward.

Those surroundings and influences are a lot to manage. Many of today's Outpacers are famous for their incredible campus environments, from gyms to restaurants, massages to hairdressers. The actual work area is packed with beanbags, table tennis tables, snack bars and soft furnishings, full of color, comfort and modern design. All of that has a significant influence on team members. They feel cared for and comfortable, in a vibrant and fun atmosphere, which positively contributes to their motivation and is highly likely to be consistent with the way they treat the end customer.

Leadership and the influence it exerts come heavily into play when building the right environment. The values will have been set out along with the mVision, but it is the way those values are demonstrated by leaders on a daily basis that creates the environment. Are they empowering or are they controlling? Do they blame employees if something goes wrong or try to understand how it happened so they can stop it from happening again? Do they pat team members on the back after a job well done or encourage them to reach beyond the goal they have set themselves? All of these actions have a massive impact on the environment that is created.

Amazon and Netflix have different management mantras, keys to success and values, which are 100 per cent authentic to the individual business. They are clear, easy to follow and have made a massive contribution to the legendary environments in both organizations that is undoubtedly critical to their ongoing Outpacer status.

Jeff Bezos sets out four principles within Amazon's core values:

customer obsession, long-term thinking, eagerness to invent and taking pride in operational excellence. "We go back to them over and over again," he says. "And if you look through each thing that we do, you will see them run straight through everything." The Amazon environment is a direct result of the consistency with which these values are demonstrated on a daily basis by leadership. It's no accident.

Netflix's corporate website openly talks about its management philosophy, the culture and the values that its leadership displays. For more of the background, take a look at Reed's brilliant book *No Rules Rules*. When it comes to environment, Netflix has created something unique, envied and enduring.

Remember, what Netflix and Amazon do are brilliant reference points, but your environment and culture will need to be unique and authentic to you. To be an Outpacer, I believe you need to create an environment that attracts and develops talent that will be devoted, which will then feed into a positive workplace culture.

I was struck by some great research on the qualities of a positive workplace culture, published in the Harvard Business Review by Emma Seppälä and Kim Cameron. Looking at their research, I can see the overlap between those qualities and the kind of environment found within the Outpacer. If you've selected the right talent, there's a lot less "ass whipping" required to get a group of individuals to perform at the highest levels. Seppälä and Cameron identified six essential characteristics of a positive workplace culture and I think they are a really helpful guide to the environment you need within an Outpacer:

1. Caring for, being interested in and maintaining responsibility for colleagues as friends.

2. Providing support for one another, including offering kindness and compassion when others are struggling.
3. Avoiding blame and forgiving mistakes.
4. Inspiring one another at work.
5. Emphasizing the meaningfulness of the work.
6. Treating one another with respect, gratitude, trust and integrity.

To the skeptic, these traits might appear too soft and hardly likely to encourage high performance. But remember that if you've recruited the best talent on the planet, you want the behaviors above to be displayed by everyone, ensuring that the environment that your talent devotes so much of its time and effort to is a highly positive one. It doesn't mean avoiding performance conversations or not addressing issues, it just means that when you do, there's no need to be an idiot about it. Agreed, an Outpacer is not an environment that will put up with carrying deadwood. But if the need arises, respectfully investigate why someone's performance is not where it should be and do all you can to give that individual the opportunity to show why you spent all that time, money and effort recruiting them in the first place. If it's not to be, the faster that is (mutually, if possible) decided, the better.

Devoted talent wants to interact and connect with other devoted talent. As the group gets bigger, your business not only becomes a more attractive place to work, but also a stronger and more powerful environment, better able to achieve the mVision.

OWNERSHIP

There's no doubt that a sense of ownership is a key part of inspiring devotion in your talent. While owning a financial stake in the organization where you work is a motivator for many, we are talking about more than just financial incentives. The more an employee feels that they are trusted to take ownership of decision-making, the more engaged they are and the harder they will work. To be an Outpacer you need to maximize productivity, so individuals and teams that have the desire to put forth their best effort are critical and of huge benefit.

Most of us have heard of or seen "helicopter parents" in action. With (mostly) the best of intentions, the parent holds on to ownership of every aspect of a situation their child is in. The message that the parent sends out is that they are in charge and taking responsibility. The flip side is the child often reacts by taking no responsibility and no care in decision-making, knowing that the parent is there to save the day.

Unfortunately, the same is true in many traditional corporates, where you will find what I call the "helicopter manager". The situations may be somewhat different but the outcome is the same – individuals take less responsibility and don't put enough care and thought into decision-making. Sadly, it becomes contagious and can lead to what some have labelled "learnt helplessness", where everyone looks for someone else to take on issues and solve problems, instead of having a sense of ownership and a desire to solve it for themselves.

Have you ever been in a restaurant or hotel and had an issue that needs resolving? You ask a member of staff for help, but all you get is a blank look and the phrase: "That's not my job." You raise your eyes to heaven in frustration, and your perception of the establishment drops considerably. The opposite experience is also true. If that member of staff can help, you feel grateful, impressed and more likely to return.

In an Outpacer, everyone feels that sense of ownership, and not just of their own work. They feel a sense of ownership of the whole organization. An Outpacer empowers its people to take action and solve problems, knowing that they hired great people who make great decisions to achieve the mVision.

When things go wrong, which they will, that individual will feel a sense of responsibility to fix the problem. And they won't be on their own. They can look to their teammates, who will be happy to lend a hand and take pride in getting it sorted, knowing the favor will be returned if and when it's required down the line.

CHALLENGE

The challenge has got to be great. This is very much the translation of the mVision down to the individual level and it provides the kind of motivation and stimulation that are essential to fueling devoted talent.

Having goals that are transparent and aligned right across the organization is important and powerful. It breaks down silos and ensures that you are truly harnessing that devoted talent you've worked so hard to recruit and to motivate each day to go after the challenge that's been set.

Google make each employee's objectives and key results accessible to everyone. You can just click on a name and find out what their goals are. This level of transparency is a must if you want to build trust and get everyone to pull together. It also helps to see that everyone else you're working with also has seriously challenging goals, as it allows everyone to see the importance and ambition of what is being attempted. You can see how each person and every team is pulling together to overcome great challenges on the way to achieving their goal and that of their team in order to help the overall organization achieve the mVision.

ENGAGEMENT

Once you've done the hard work of selecting and recruiting your devoted talent, you've got to nurture and grow them. Think of your talent as an organism that needs certain nutrients to be at its best. Engagement provides vital nourishment and is a hallmark of the Outpacer. The energy derived from a united sense of purpose creates constant engagement, which becomes an engine driving all aspects of the organization.

One of the misconceptions is that an Outpacer should be a cut-throat environment. In fact, as I outlined earlier, the opposite is true: a positive and supportive environment is crucial. A culture of fear can create engagement (and sometimes even excitement) for a short period, but research suggests that the inevitable stress it creates will likely lead to disengagement over the long term. Engagement in work – which is associated with feeling valued, secure, supported and respected – is generally negatively associated with a high-stress, cut-throat culture.

Disengagement is also costly. In studies by the Queen's School of Business and by the Gallup Organization, disengaged workers had 37 per cent higher absenteeism, 49 per cent more accidents and 60 per cent more errors and defects. Organizations with low employee engagement scores experienced 18 per cent lower productivity, 16 per cent lower profitability, 37 per cent lower job growth and 65 per cent lower share price over time. Importantly, businesses with highly engaged employees enjoyed 100 per cent more job applications.

The old mantra "Communicate, communicate, communicate" needs to be alive and present in an Outpacer. Devoted talent should feel like a critical contributor to the journey, which is an exciting adventure for everyone. Each step towards the ultimate mVision should be shared across the organization, in a careful balance of sharing tactical progress day-to-day while also celebrating monumental moments that are the bigger steps towards the ultimate goal.

Don't brush failures under the carpet or over-celebrate success. At Outpacers there's always more to be done, so there should be no room for either complacency or a whiff of arrogance to emerge.

At an Outpacer, everyone needs to be driving forwards together with the same level of commitment. Part of that collective march is a common belief that every step matters and every detail is important. This is a direct result of great engagement – feeling valued, knowing your contribution is making a difference and seeing it in action, with the most effective visualization being, of course, seeing the customer impact of your work.

As we will cover in Chapter 9 on Customer Experience, it is critical that your engagement strategy for employees is consistent with the customer engagement strategy. The way you treat your people will have a direct correlation to the way they treat your customers. For example, Outpacers have employee journeys mapped out alongside customer journeys, which have the same lofty goals and ambitions, with a consistent set of values.

Empowerment is all important. At the Outpacer, the ability to get things done without lengthy instruction is a core capability. Individuals should be clear about how their role, goals and objectives contribute to the overall trajectory of the business. Their contribution should be appreciated and recognized, allowing them to unleash their talent while relishing the fact that what they do really matters.

Finally, don't forget to be human. Make sure you're having fun, and that all the people around you are too. In the Outpacer, the leader sets the tone, making sure there are opportunities to relax, unwind, get to know colleagues on a deeper level and blow off some steam. And while we know these are best done in person, Covid-19 has allowed the Outpacers to explore virtual experiences that achieve a great outcome. They may often be for shorter lengths of time, but they can be done more frequently. In the Outpacer, happiness and fulfillment are core elements of the engagement equation.

ACHIEVEMENT

Recognition by peers, receipt of patents, or just being part of something that is purposeful is really important; because achievements matter to top talent.

Achievement of the mVision has to bring reward. That reward might be fame amongst the engineering community, or it might be making the front page of the *Financial Times*. Ultimately, high achievement is likely to translate into an increase in an individual's personal wealth. For some, money is an important goal, while for others it's more a fair, logical and just distribution of the financial success they've worked so hard to achieve. Some buy a McLaren, some share it with their families, others give it to charity . . . and some do all three!

DEVELOPMENT

Development (or progression) is a key ingredient for the environment in which devoted talent wants to reside. They won't tolerate standing still either personally or professionally, and that puts a huge positive strain on the organization to keep everything moving with significant momentum.

At a personal level, development encompasses both physical and mental wellbeing. Employees will look to build emotional intelligence, communication skills, rapport and confidence. They might want to learn a new language, or improve physical development in fitness and sport, as well as relaxing and recharging the mind through yoga and/or Pilates. You might think of these as fads and a waste of money., but your devoted talent is leaving the beehive to become stronger, more resilient and more thoughtful. Encourage it and reap the benefits.

Professionally, there needs to be a clear career trajectory. Top talent wants to move forward, progressing to ever more important roles with greater accountability for the achievement of the mVision. Coaching is a critical intervention to help ensure they are on the right path and that they are maximizing their talent and energy.

Like anyone who's on top of their game, the best didn't get there by luck. It took hard work and that work ethic remains. So exceptional training is a must to keep these individuals at peak performance. The Outpacer takes training as seriously as any top-flight sports team.

As part of the development culture, there also needs to be a recognition of those who aren't performing to the standard required. Even if their performance is up to standard, if they are the wrong fit culturally, they can be causing huge damage. Former England rugby coach Sir Clive Woodward describes how the words of a marine helped him shape the 2003 World Cup-winning team: "It's not about the skills. It's about attitude and the effect on the team. One wrong team player can sap all the energy from the group." Sir Clive went on to kick any "energy sappers" off the squad, no matter how talented they were, and replace them with "energizers".

It's also important to recognize that people have skills and capabilities that are necessary for certain periods in an organization's evolution. When the needs change, so does the kind of talent required to drive performance. It's absolutely right to invest in and develop individuals so that they can perform in the new environment. It's equally important to call it when it's not working (for both the individual and the organization).

In conclusion, to have devoted talent, your selection has to be flawless and your ongoing performance management rigorous and

MARC BENIOFF

Marc Benioff co-founded Salesforce, a customer relationship management (CRM) system with a groundbreaking twist, in 1999. All the software and critical customer data would be in the cloud and made available as a subscription service. This pioneering "software as a service" model quickly spread across the technology industry. Since then it has outpaced almost everyone, with an average annual growth of 29.1 per cent, while creating a culture that has attracted and retained talent that is truly devoted.

Marc is a larger than life character with passion and charisma on full display 24/7. It's easy to see why he's attracted some of the best talent in the world. Salesforce personifies devoted talent, nailing the eight elements discussed above. It has created an environment where the best of the best are devoted, loving what they do and pursuing purposeful goals that drive a sense of fulfillment at an individual and team level.

As an archetypal leader of an Outpacer, Marc's passion for performance and impact extends beyond products and services into society, and that's a big part of the dedicated following he's created. Three core elements that have been there since day one create the fertile ground for devoted talent to thrive.

Firstly, you have the "Ohana" spirit, a support system nurtured inside the company, derived from the traditional Hawaiian philosophy of family and the way in which families are bound together and responsible for one another. It extends from employees to customers, partners, developers and members of Salesforce's communities. It determines how colleagues work collaboratively, take care of one another and have fun together!

Secondly, the 1-1-1 philanthropic model was another of Marc's building blocks. When the company was founded, it committed to putting 1 per cent of its equity into the Salesforce Foundation. Each year it allocates 1 per cent of its employees' time to volunteer work and it donates 1 per cent of its product to nonprofits.

Thirdly, there is the culture. Salesforce treats its employees fairly and puts a lot of effort into making sure all employees are valued and rewarded. Marc set out a very strong mVision, with clear responsibility to live out and uphold the company values of "Trust, Customer Success, Innovation and Equality". Salesforce's leaders put their people first and empower them to get things done

Wrap these three together and you have something very powerful. Alongside its commercial success and massive philanthropic contribution, Salesforce regularly features as one of the best workplaces in the corporate world, with a long list of accolades and a decent-sized trophy cabinet!

Get a ticket for the Dreamforce conference, the huge star-sprinkled celebration/trade show/retreat that Salesforce throws every year, and you'll hear from Marc that business is the greatest platform for change. It's clear that this forms part of what makes Salesforce such a special place to work and why those who do work there give everything they've got to achieve the mission.

Unlike some CEOs, Marc's commitment to social and environmental causes is passionate and authentic. "He wrote the book on stakeholder capitalism," says Klaus Schwab, the founder of the World Economic Forum, meaning it both metaphorically and literally, given the several books Benioff has written. His New York Times Bestseller *Trailblazer* is described as delivering "an inspiring vision for successful companies of the future – in which changing the world is everyone's business".

I've been around the corporate world long enough to know that nowhere is perfect. But you'll never get close to perfect unless you try to establish a strong element of purpose outside of the business goals, and have some real fun (full-on party with your friends fun, not that cringey corporate fun day nonsense!). Mix this with the humility to know there's always room to be better and you create a great place to work and the environment for devoted talent to thrive.

GRETA THUNBERG

Environmentalists have been campaigning about climate change for years with a low to medium impact. Then came 15-year-old Greta Thunberg, protesting outside the Swedish parliament to pressure the government to meet carbon emissions targets. Her small campaign had a global effect, inspiring young people across the world to organize their own strikes. From the UK to Japan, millions joined her by skipping school to protest and a year later, she received the first of three Nobel Peace Prize nominations for climate activism. How did this schoolgirl punch through the resistance layer and create a movement of devoted talent that wants to pursue her mission?

Greta Thunberg has a bundle of qualities that we should all emulate: she's authentic, passionate, energetic, caring, committed, brave, selfless, calls everyone out (from presidents to me and you), uses data and facts, gets to the right places and addresses all her audiences, from youth to the Davos elite to the UN, who she powerfully told:

"My message is that we'll be watching you. This is all wrong. I shouldn't be up here. I should be back in school on the other side of the ocean. Yet you all come to us young people for hope. How dare you. You have stolen my dreams and my childhood with your empty words."

She's taken a topic (climate change) that seemed to still be up for debate, and through her tireless commitment and communication skills, moved the dial from debate to action. You could say that she's had truth on her side, but so did those who went before.

Thunberg seems to get the balance between pushing right to the line of inspiration, but not going beyond it where some could accuse her of being fanatical or out of touch with reality. Ultimately she's created a movement with a mass following. If she was a business with revenue, she'd be on the front cover of Fortune.

Like another Outpacer, Elon Musk, she too has been diagnosed with Asperger's syndrome (a form of autism). Rather than viewing it as an illness, she has described it as her superpower and used the hashtag #aspiepower. She says that being on the autism spectrum makes you different and in a crisis being different helps you think outside the box, making her "a good resource". Her vulnerability, honesty and authenticity are compelling.

She and Marc Benioff are two very different people, but they both attract and drive devoted talent in a way that few before them have managed to achieve. Certainly, one of the lessons is that you can't fake this stuff – if you try, you'll be found out very quickly. To outpace, see your position in the world as part of an ecosystem – you cannot operate in isolation from everything else. You have to be outpacing on all fronts, and only then will you get the talent you need that's ready and able to change the world.

As I've covered, for me work–life balance is no longer a valid aim. I believe we have a work–life blend; Bezos calls it a circle. What matters to the best talent isn't neatly compartmentalized, meaning that as an employer you need to appeal to the whole person and what matters to them in and out of work. If you want the best, you need to use business as a platform for change. You need to create a strong purpose for people to want to be really with you on your mVision. Therefore, those outside of the traditional business context, like Thunberg, who are able to create huge followings and have monumental impact on the world have much to teach us and we have much to learn.

CHAPTER 4

COLLABORATIVE INNOVATION

What does that really mean?

Collaborative innovation is not an initiative or transformation project, but rather an enterprise-wide capability and approach. Employees, business partners, customers and stakeholders are encouraged to suggest and develop new innovative ideas, which are then peer reviewed and tested – only the strongest survive. The north star for all new innovations is for them to materially move the business forward in line with the mVision and rapidly impact the market. Collaboration is at the heart of the innovation approach. Internal silos are knocked down to get the best from teams within the business, while partnering and exploring with third parties is encouraged to bring new perspectives and capabilities, ultimately enhancing the creativity, innovation and impact.

Why is this important?

You can't be an Outpacer without innovation at the heart of your business. It's not one person's job; collaboration is at the heart of everyone's job, and it's not something you can put on the annual schedule.

Outpacers know that innovation isn't simply about investing in the latest technologies. It's about improving today's products and creating new business models and ideas that allow real disruption and generate opportunities for growth. Outpacers tend to take a much more strategic approach to the way they embed and encourage innovation across the organization and seek out new partners and opportunities for collaboration. They align their innovation investments with their mVision to develop audacious strategies that generate new value and drive future growth.

Innovation is a hard thing to visualize. If pushed, people might imagine a scientist in a lab coat, or a couple of coders on their laptops in a dark room. At an Outpacer, I see people bound by a common mVision and desire to make something better. Most great innovations were not created by an individual; they were an output of collaboration – often within an entrepreneurial culture, by devoted people, pushing towards a clear mVision.

Innovation is a must for the Outpacer. It's often a key part of where they've come from and something of which they're extremely proud. But, a bit like that often elusive second album, Outpacers need to work hard to ensure innovation is a part of every day, versus a one-off moment of genius. Longevity in business is a hallmark of true greatness.

Innovation and invention are not the same

Some people mistakenly believe that innovation and invention are the same thing. They are not. An invention is a thing or an item, for example, the smartphone. An innovation is more about how you use that item. Often that results in changes in behavior, with an outcome that is widely believed to be better than before.

Take the iPhone. I wouldn't say that Apple invented the smartphone, as there were many before Apple entered the market. IBM is widely credited with developing the world's first smartphone, which it called Simon. It went on sale in 1994 and featured a touchscreen, email capability and a handful of built-in apps, including a calculator and a sketch pad. And don't forget BlackBerry. At its peak in 2012, there were 77 million BlackBerry subscribers, but ultimately it wasn't able to hold on to its one-time market-leading position. So the iPhone may not have been the first smartphone, but it's grown to be one of the best and most popular.

I would argue the iPhone was more an innovation than an invention. In fact, I'd go further and say that it is the epitome of what I mean by collaborative innovation. Not only did it take the very best of the incredible innovation for which Apple is world renowned, but the company also collaborated with third-party app developers to bring the iPhone's capability to life. That internal and external collaborative innovation led to arguably one of the greatest products of all time.

That's why the power of collaborative innovation is so important to creating an Outpacer: it's the scale opportunity that comes with changes in behavior and/or interactions with millions or even billions of people. And it doesn't stop at that one great innovation. Again, look at the iPhone. When I recently showed my kids my old iPhone 1, they didn't actually know what it was! That's how much Apple has pushed itself to innovate since creating the first iPhone. You've got to keep innovating to remain on top.

Should you be a first mover or fast follower?

It's a question that people love to debate. Should you be an organization that takes a product or service to market first? Or be a fast follower, a company that is quick to pick up good new ideas from other companies?

If you're hoping for a definitive answer, I'm afraid you're going to be disappointed. I actually don't think it matters. Neither approach works unless you embed collaborative innovation at the heart of your organization. If you are a first mover and you don't innovate what you've brought to market, you will be overtaken by a fast follower. And if you're that fast follower and you don't further innovate, you too will be overtaken.

So forget about the debate and instead focus on collaborative innovation. Outpacers, like great athletes, don't stand still. They keep pushing and improving to sustain their advantage.

A tablespoon of paranoia, no ego

Early Outpacers often originally used an innovation to usurp an established player or create a new, huge, untapped market. Those now established Outpacers find themselves looking over their shoulders at others wanting to take their crown. To be a great Outpacer, a healthy amount of paranoia is, in fact, very helpful. The minute complacency sets in, someone will pass you in the fast lane to market dominance.

As well as having a decent dose of healthy paranoia, Outpacers are full of people who leave ego at the door and love to explore ideas and options with other talented individuals. I often describe Outpacers as intellectually curious.

Sir Alex Ferguson, legendary former manager of Manchester United, was famous for saying, "Nobody is bigger than the club." There were many individual footballing greats that played on his teams, but when he thought their ego or belief in themselves got in the way of the team chemistry, he would trade them in a heartbeat. I would say that Sir Alex's hostility to individualism was similar to the environment at an Outpacer.

Outpacers love to collaborate and often those favoring the solo approach are rejected. (SpaceX has the not so subtle "no asshole rule", which governs its hiring, firing and promotion policies. People who interrupt others, shut down conversations and create a hostile environment that prevents collaboration are weeded out.) The old adage "two heads are better than one" is of course true and not lost on those in an Outpacer. And this ethos sits at the heart of the approach to innovation. Working together, iterating and constantly trying to perfect is the norm.

The Open Source initiative is a great example of the power of collaborative innovation. Without it, Linux, which at one point powered 95 per cent of the top 500 most powerful supercomputers in the world, wouldn't exist.

Open Source is a vast open forum of innovators happy to share their knowledge in a collaborative environment to create new opportunities for the greater good. Hugely talented individuals work together under a clearly defined framework, allowing them to collaborate and push the boundaries of what's possible through their collective capabilities. Often those working together are not bound by a single company mVision. Engineers are happy to share their ideas outside the limited confines of their organizations and have others improve on them. In fact, Linux has 18,000 contributing companies. What binds contributors is the challenge of driving innovation, working with great people and doing something that will be beneficial to the tech sector and even mankind. It's proof of the power of many coming together with a common mission and is certainly not the place for ego-maniacs seeking solo glory.

The mergers and acquisitions debate

The outpacing world really is survival of the fittest. Think of an Outpacer as a thriving wild animal on the Serengeti, where it's eat or be eaten! The greatest competitors will do whatever it takes to win. As we've talked about, there is often very little ego in an Outpacer, which looks for inspiration everywhere. They're not so complacent as to think that they have all the answers, or that no one else can do it better than them. They also understand the concept of speed and scale. If they can acquire something or a group of people that will allow them to be more innovative faster than they can manage organically, they press the button and get it done.

While you'll find copious data points that say lots of mergers and acquisitions fail, I'd argue, as someone who's been on every conceivable side of inorganic activity – being acquired, doing the acquiring and as an advisor to clients on both the buy and sell sides – that good deals with good people (and good advisors!) go well. Today's Outpacers have thrived from the M&A they've done. Just look at YouTube, Instagram, Android, Ring, Whole Foods, Beats or Intel's modem business. There's no doubt in my mind that M&A can play a vital role in driving innovation at an Outpacer.

This section is not intended to be an M&A handbook. There are certainly many things that you need to get right for a successful integration, too many to cover here. But one thing I would highlight is the importance of not demotivating the internal team with any kind of unintended messaging that says "you're not good enough" (unless that's the message you want to send). As long as you're treating your devoted talent in the right way, engaging them all the time, they too will welcome the innovation, market edge and greater shot of nailing the mVision that will come from the M&A activity.

One final word on the growing debate about M&A stifling competition: Stratechery's Ben Thompson has called Facebook's acquisition of Instagram "the greatest regulatory failure of the past decade". Competition regulation has always been important to the overall economy of any country, and if regulators see the need to set new precedents and create new laws, they will. Today's Outpacers are very much following the free market principles on which the economies where they operate were founded. So while the debate rages on whether M&A is right or wrong for today's most notorious Outpacers, I'd simply say that both M&A and vibrant competition are crucial, and those able to master collaborative innovation are most likely to come out on top.

So how do you do it?

To achieve true collaborative innovation as an Outpacer, I'd suggest five key things on which to focus:

NORTH STAR

Provide clear focus and direction so that as your people collaborate and innovate, they are following the same path and getting you closer to your mVision.

In its early days, Google was famous for its "20 per cent time" policy, which allowed its engineers to spend 20 per cent of their time on personal projects. The policy is said to have resulted in some of the company's most successful products, such as Gmail, AdSense and Google Talk.

But as Google grew it reined in this policy and replaced it with a more focused approach to innovation that emphasized bigger teams working together with greater focus. In 2011, CEO Larry Page announced that Google would adopt a "more wood behind fewer arrows" strategy that would put more of Google's resources and employees behind a smaller number of projects. In his words, "focus and prioritization are crucial given our amazing opportunities".

At the time, some observers speculated on the potential negative impact the end of "20 per cent time" would have. In fact, Google's value has more than tripled since then. The new approach of "more wood behind fewer arrows" clearly worked! Googlers have been given a clear north star and it ensures that the company is investing in and supporting innovation in all the right areas without getting distracted. This greater focus has not limited creativity. It's still possible to be creative and innovative, and for them to have conversations with colleagues that inspire, within the goals that have been set. It's simply that all that energy and creativity that could previously fire off in any direction is now driven into focused areas. Celebrate that focus and ensure that everyone understands why "no" is sometimes the right answer.

EVERYONE'S JOB

Unless collaborative innovation is a part of everyone's job, it simply isn't going to happen in a way that will ensure you become an Outpacer. Some companies create a "transformation team" to drive change. The message that can be subliminally sent to everyone is that no one other than that team has responsibility for transformation – so everyone else just cracks on with their day jobs! Transformation needs to be everyone's job or it won't happen. The same is true with innovation. It's not something that can be outsourced or given to a team. It needs to be part of the fabric of the organization.

If it's part of everyone's job, then it needs to be a part of everyone's goals and objectives, and be embedded in the overall performance management. And no, not twice a year in performance reviews. At an Outpacer, the innovation discussion should be a constant. Take my definition of collaborative innovation and ask the question: "How have you worked with others to take something and change how it's used, with an outcome that is widely believed to be better than before?"

At the most basic of levels, there is power in simply asking the question to everyone in an organization. If you're trying to get things moving in a less than innovative environment, leadership needs to be asking that question all the time, and then celebrating and rewarding those who model the right behavior. Everyone will soon understand what's expected and how to move forward in the organization. Those that don't need to find somewhere else to make a living.

BE INSPIRED

At the Outpacer, inspiration can come from many places. The intellectual curiosity that is so often on display leads people to be constantly on the hunt for new ideas and ways of doing things.

According to Steve Jobs, at Apple "innovation comes from people meeting up in the hallways or calling each other at 10:30 at night with a new idea, or because they realized something that shoots holes in how we've been thinking about a problem".

While inspiration can come from anywhere and everywhere, I'd suggest five key sources for you to constantly scour: colleagues, customers, competitors, third parties and straight out of left field.

The key to inspiration is being open to it in the first place. For devoted talent, that drive to be the best means that they are pushing every day and inspiring all around them to be the best. They don't just sit around and accept the status quo. They push their **colleagues** and question how that team can work together to innovate and get to the mVision better and faster.

We haven't specifically talked about environment in this chapter, but it's clearly very important. You need to create situations for colleagues to share informally. Eric Schmidt and Jonathan Rosenberg explain how it works at Google. "It's best to work in small teams, keep them crowded and foster serendipitous connections." Sometimes, the best inspiration comes when you least expect it.

Science fiction writer Isaac Asimov wrote a letter in 1959 as part of a group conducting research for the US government's Advanced Research Projects Agency (ARPA), recommending "cerebration sessions" to promote innovation beyond invention. He said that shared thinking and informal collaboration were key components of problem solving and accelerating change. He suggested that cerebration sessions could be used to "group think" new ideas, new possibilities and new combinations of knowledge and experience, which could find new answers and new directions. The concept of inspiration from colleagues clearly isn't new, but for it to move from theory to reality, your people have to be open and ready to let their minds go to work with others.

Outpacers don't spend time guessing what their **customers** want. They combine deep market insights – informed by real-time customer data – with their belief in their mVision to constantly measure impact and identify opportunities to satisfy unmet customer needs, even "nudging" customers to alter their buying habits. This allows an Outpacer to seemingly deliver what customers don't even know they want yet. When Amazon first let customers post reviews of products in 1995, many people thought the company had lost the plot. But on the contrary, it turned the feedback into gold by acting upon the findings.

It was an innovation that made Amazon better. Customers are a great source of inspiration.

Very few people would dispute that **competition** drives innovation. So don't just hate on the competition. Instead think about how they can inspire your business to be better. To be an Outpacer you need to be competitive and there are often huge things to learn (both good and bad) from watching those with whom you do battle in the market.

I'm a great believer in the benefit of having **third parties** offering different perspectives and experiences that provide inspiration to the innovation process. While I really do believe that within an Outpacer the boundaries of innovation can be pushed and stretched, I also think that third parties can help eliminate the challenges associated with groupthink. This is certainly where the benefits of corporate incubators or ventures can be distributed across the organization (see p. 84 for more on external collaboration).

Finally, sometimes that inspiration can come when you least expect it, **straight out of left field**. Maybe it's from your friends or family, maybe it's when you've taken time out for yourself, or maybe it's when you're on holiday. Often it comes during a break from your regular environment, and results from diversity of thought or practice. You are in a place that is alien, and the people you're engaging with aren't like you. Their thought process is different and they see things differently. That's a great time to be inspired, just as long as you're open to it. #noego!

HEALTH AND SAFETY

Don't worry, this is not about high-visibility jackets and hard hats! When I say health and safety in the context of collaborative innovation, I mean ensuring that it's a healthy approach where all individuals feel safe and want to participate.

Again, this is not a new concept. Isaac Asimov went beyond talking about cerebration processes and outlined the importance of a safe environment for innovation to take place. He said, "First and foremost, there must be ease, relaxation and a general sense of permissiveness. The world in general disapproves of creativity, and to be creative in public is particularly bad. Even to speculate in public is rather worrisome. The individuals must, therefore, have the feeling that the others won't object."

Bear in mind, this was the late 1950s, so things have clearly changed – I certainly think you're pretty safe to speculate in public nowadays! But the point is a good one. You're not going to get the best from your people if they don't trust you and feel safe. You have to encourage, almost cajole the input and ideas from everyone. It's not just those who shout loudest. In a truly collaborative environment, input must be sought from everyone and value ascribed to everything that goes into the melting pot of innovation.

It helps to have tools that allow everyone to communicate strategically about innovation. Good ideas can come from anywhere, but would-be innovators may need help developing a strong strategic argument.

Amazon's approach to meetings is well documented, with its six-page memo (the narrative structure of which, according to Bezos "forces better thought and better understanding of scope") and internal press release – both required reading for all meeting participants – almost as famous as Bezos himself. The approach isn't specifically for decisions on innovation, but many of Amazon's best advances have benefited from highly productive, strategic meetings using the memo and press release, where the customer was put front and center and a great innovation brought to life.

Amazon insider Brittain Ladd has talked about the value of this process. He explains that the approach was: "If it was hard to write a press release or understand why a product or service would add value to customers, the product or service wasn't worth the effort." When creating Amazon Prime, Amazon knew that customers wanted to buy quality products for less money, and to receive them as fast as possible. "An internal press release was written centered around the existing problem (high costs, slow deliveries), why current solutions had failed to correct the problem, and how the new product (Prime) would blow away all existing solutions," explains Ladd. This was accompanied by a six-page memo detailing logistical, product and budgetary issues. The clarity of purpose provided by each meant that strategic decisions on the viability and implementation of Prime could be made confidently, and the innovation brought to the market quickly.

While it's important to have some structure, it mustn't stifle the very creativity that it's there to facilitate. A good governance model (which we will cover in more detail in Chapter 8) should enable the right things to get through. It's not there to stop failure at all costs. Companies excelling at collaborative innovation fail all the time, but they take the learnings and incorporate them into the next innovation. It's cultural "no fear"!

As Elon Musk says, "Failure is an option here. If things are not failing, you are not innovating enough."

WEIGHTS AND MEASURES

How do you put the right measurement around innovation? Management thinker Peter Drucker is often quoted as saying that "you can't manage what you can't measure". To a large degree, I think that is true. But an obsessive approach to trying to measure the impact of collaborative innovation may just strangle the creativity that it's trying to foster.

You could certainly consider measuring innovation by traditional means such as annual R&D budget as a percentage of sales, number of patents filed, or percentage of sales from new products. But I'm not convinced this is the way to go. Blackberry had 40,000 patents, but that didn't help it over the long term.

In a sense, the danger is that by trying to shoe-horn innovation into traditional metrics you over-complicate what you're attempting to do. If innovation is a fundamental part of your business fabric, then you don't necessarily need a bunch of new metrics to measure it. Remember that an Outpacer is constantly innovating everything. The algorithms at Facebook or Google are changing and improving all the time. That change wouldn't be classed as a new product, but it is innovation and it's achieved by teams collaborating together.

Think about it this way: if you look at your market share by product, customer satisfaction scores or your growth rate, you'll get a pretty good indication as to whether your customers/users see you as innovative. If you want greater details, look at your return on capital employed. Are you really investing in the right areas? If so, you'll be achieving market-leading returns. And how about this as a scary concept: ask your people and your customers. Use a system similar to a Net Promoter Score (NPS), a metric that measures (on a scale of 0–10) customer loyalty and satisfaction. If you're not getting an 8 or above, you're not innovative. What score out of 10 would you give Apple, Amazon, Netflix, Google or Facebook for innovation? There's a reason why they're worth an astonishing $5 trillion.

A little help from friends (and frenemies) . . .

Collaboration and innovation from within are essential, but there's no need (and in many cases no benefit) to going it alone. The iPhone is fantastic, but one of its critical success factors is the apps, many of which are not developed by Apple. At first glance it seems bizarre that Apple would allow a Kindle app in its app store, or that Amazon would release a version of its Kindle reader to Apple for the iPad, but both parties know that in this instance, there's more to be gained than lost. Outpacers have learnt not to be a closed shop or a walled garden, but instead to open themselves up to collaboration even with organizations who they might think of as enemies, now considered frenemies.

Collaboration with third parties can take many forms. Outpacers are adept at knowing when to tap into the expertise of others who can provide complementary non-core capabilities. Take Amazon's investment in start-up electric car manufacturer Rivian. Rather than building its own fleet of electric vehicles, which it would have had the capability to do, Amazon invested in Rivian and committed to buying thousands of electric vehicles from them. The agreement allowed the smaller company to build highly innovative battery technology and Amazon to have a more environmentally friendly delivery fleet, while remaining focused on its core mission. It resisted the temptation that some of the biggest companies fall into to do everything themselves, and instead used capital to invest in other companies that are developing non-core capabilities.

Another Outpacer trait is to invest in emerging technologies, which provides both a seat on the board and access to developments that they might want to adopt. This works well for more developed Outpacers with funding capacity. Smaller wannabe Outpacers might not have the capital to invest but a more collaborative partnership model, in which both parties are contributing, can equally create opportunities in the market for both.

If you weren't lucky enough to be part of an epic and innovative company from the outset, you may find yourself part of an organization that is struggling to innovate at all. Even large organizations that have veered off course can think about how to collaborate with other businesses to drive innovative performance. Some CEOs look to address the innovation underperformance by setting up a corporate accelerator or venture arm.

The advantage here is that the smaller start-up can come in and transfer knowledge on the way it develops innovation and product that is different from the approach taken by the "mother ship". Exposure to these differences allows people to open their eyes to new ways of working and to experiment with some of the methods the smaller business uses.

While I'd advocate any form of collaboration with third parties, it's important to ensure that it's integrated into the core business and that everyone feels engaged. The Harvard Business Review published research looking at why almost three quarters of corporate innovation initiatives fail to deliver the desired results. Unsurprisingly, they found that it wasn't necessarily the innovation itself that wasn't working, but the lack of collaboration and integration within the broader business. One of their main insights and suggested strategies was to "boost the value of venturing to the rest of the business". They found business directors can be unwilling to collaborate with the corporate venturing unit because they fail to understand the strategic value of working with a start-up and instead remain wedded to their traditional performance metrics. Internal politics then become the deathknell to the venture.

One possibility is to use a third party to collaborate on innovation within one specific product group. In this scenario, it won't be the case that the entire employee base is involved. But such an approach can be publicly championed and used to accelerate the use of collaboration innovation with third parties within other product groups, on the way to getting the whole organization on board. You would engage your people by sharing the north star that was being focused on, how the team went about it, what they learnt, what they achieved and how it can be replicated by others.

There's no one size fits all. There are many ways to approach collaborative innovation, and sometimes a mix of approaches works. Big corporations may take the dual approach of fostering a collaborative culture internally while also working with smaller innovative companies already in that space, particularly if their own culture has some way to go. Realistically, developing an outpacing collaborative innovation culture won't happen overnight. It's all well and good being purist in approach, but working with smaller, more innovative companies might be the more pragmatic option for some on the road to Outpacer status.

. . . and suppliers

Getting the best out of your supply chain is very important. One of the interesting things is how to structure contracts to incentivize suppliers to be innovative. Continually investing in and improving a service provided by a supplier doesn't necessarily form part of the contract, but Outpacers will make sure that this happens. One option is to create an innovation fund where suppliers are pushed to create a pool of funding to provide innovation to the products or services they provide, or it's agreed that both parties will contribute, which is then directed by the stakeholders involved into whatever will help push the boundaries of innovation and improve the service. Contracts around digital services and user interfaces, for example, might include assessments on a quarterly basis, where parameters around speed, quality or user experience might be set, and joint agreement made on where money should be spent to innovate and improve performance.

Of course it's possible to secure a contract at lower cost and perhaps even push the onus onto the supplier to fund innovation, but by coming to the party and taking equal responsibility, it's more likely that something good will follow as a result. The more input and collaboration you have, the better it will be.

Scaling up success

Having used the best of the organization's collective brainpower, the innovation that follows needs to be put to market as quickly as possible. Minimum Viable Product (MVP) is a Silicon Valley doctrine. In today's software-led environment, long gone are the days when companies would take a year to launch a new product, having developed it in a factory, tested it, sent it to user groups, refined it and tested it again. In the digital era, engineers can program a service, send it out to thousands of people and gain feedback, all within 24 hours. Rather than waiting to launch a perfect product, the business can launch an MVP that works. The user interface may not be perfect but the feedback will provide enough insight to know whether it's worth further investment. It's not that all the old steps are ignored, more that each stage is condensed. This is the way Outpacers fast-track a product to market, and the way you will need to react to keep pace. If you wait for a product to be perfect, someone else will already have launched it. Back on the Serengeti, your lunch will already have been taken and you'll have to start the hunt all over again!

It's important to understand that an MVP is not a product. It's a process that's repeated over and over again. No product is ever finished in an Outpacer. It is constantly being refined. That requires a full commitment to taking the feedback on board and making adjustments as necessary. It's hard to think of an Outpacer that doesn't operate with a high-profile constant feedback loop. With the everyday use of gamification, there's no escaping feedback in the digital economy. But it's important that you control the narrative, listen to what is being said and use it to continually improve. Don't be defensive. Even if customers are frustrated, they still want to use your service. They want it to be better and they've told you what to do. That feedback is gold dust.

The final word

Collaboration and innovation are where Outpacers measurably outperform their peers, continuously pushing the organizational innovation capability to deliver tangible outcomes from their investments. In an outpacing organization, everyone comes to work in the morning with a deep desire to change things and to try something new, taking inspiration from colleagues, customers, competitors and their environment, knowing that they are encouraged to and will be rewarded for doing so. Collaborative innovation is the beating heart of an outpacing business.

SUSAN WOJCICKI

If there is something in the water in Silicon Valley that breeds Outpacers, it certainly had a direct pipe to the inhabitants of the Wojcicki household! While this profile is all about the incredible collaborative innovation we see from Susan, CEO of YouTube, she's part of an illustrious family of high achievers (her sister, Anne, is also at the table of our Outpacer dinner, and quite frankly her whole family probably deserve an invite!).

Arguably, Susan's first collaboration was in renting out her garage to two guys working on a start-up who would contribute to her monthly mortgage bill. They just happened to be the co-founders of Google.

Susan went on to be employee 16, appointed as the first marketing manager of Google, rising to become the Senior Vice President of Advertising & Commerce. She was responsible for the design, innovation and engineering of all Google's advertising and measurement platforms at a time when advertising execs would still utter the famous words, "Half the money I spend on advertising is wasted; the trouble is I don't know which half."

We talked about the importance of weights and measures in pursuing collaborative innovation. That also lies at the heart of the revolution that's taken place in digital advertising, with the introduction of innovations like "cost per click" transforming advertising measurement. Rather than just hoping someone had seen their advert, advertisers were able to pay for a specific outcome (e.g. reaching the target audience). Under Susan's leadership, mind-blowing collaborative innovation has led to huge benefits for both the tech and advertising industries and transformed them forever.

During this journey to SVP, and while in charge of Google's video platform, Wojcicki saw the future. Despite the best efforts of her and her team, she realized a punchy start-up called YouTube was outperforming them, seeing incredible growth through user-generated content, with a tagline of "Broadcast Yourself". She could see there were new genres of content and formats that had never existed before. She inspired her fellow Googlers with her vision and convinced them to buy YouTube.

She was handed the reins to YouTube eight years later, in 2014. As she transitioned to CEO, Susan articulated a clear north star: "Our goal at YouTube is to be a platform where anyone in the world can access and share information. We want to give everyone a voice and a chance to succeed, by connecting people and opening up the world."

Today YouTube is a big part of most people's lives, with 2 billion logged-in users a month, across 100 countries, creating 500 hours of content a minute. Its innovative approach turned the video industry on its head, moving it from a model with huge industry gatekeepers preventing the masses from getting on TV, to one where anyone could easily upload a video of anything, find an audience and, for some, generate an income. Susan leads a team running a highly innovative platform that collaborates with content creators and advertisers for massive impact.

Hunter Walk, a former Googler who worked with Susan, said, "YouTube is as much a community product as it is an algorithm." And that community, which incorporates viewers, advertisers and creators, is thriving by almost any measure.

Susan is asked to talk a lot about being one of the few female CEOs in tech, or about the measures she's taking to manage and control inappropriate content on the platform. Both of these topics are critical, but rarely do we hear about her being at the center of people and industries working together on new and innovative approaches that are transforming our future. I think Susan Wojcicki is an innovator, collaborator and Outpacer who every day is writing a new path for billions around the world.

JAY-Z

Thousands of hip-hop stars have come and gone, but only a handful have used their platform to do more and become more by pushing all boundaries to one side, innovating, collaborating and outpacing the rest. In my opinion, Jay-Z stands tallest amongst them.

Whether you're a fan of hip-hop or not is irrelevant. Jay-Z optimizes the Outpacer characteristic of innovation and collaboration on stage, in the studio and in his business ventures. He has sold over 50 million albums and 75 million singles, won 23 Grammy Awards and, in June 2019, officially became the first hip-hop billionaire.

Jay-Z's ethos, "Picture the pinnacle", speaks to the importance of the north star. His goal was to make a gold album and become a millionaire at 30 years old even though, as a young Black man from the Marcy Houses Projects, unfortunately the odds of him dying or going to prison were higher. Undeterred by not being signed to a record label, he co-created his own, Roc-A-Fella Records. As he says, "when you envision your success it feels so close that you have no choice but to keep going, find creative ways to reach your goals and pretty much do the so-called impossible. Don't picture a little success, dream BIG! Picture it, see it, believe it."

The challenge of longevity in the music business is well known, and Jay-Z describes how success can bring fear of taking an alternative direction when the current approach works so well. As the saying goes, "If it ain't broke, don't fix it!" Whatever fears he may have had, one of the hallmarks of his greatness has been his continual innovation of his music and the world of hip-hop, including collaborations with artists from different genres that have further enhanced his reputation as a genius – from Chris Martin, Lenny Kravitz and Linkin Park to Kanye

West, Alicia Keys and of course his wife Beyoncé. He's clear on his intention when it comes to collaboration, which is to maintain a sense of yourself and not try to copy the other party. Rather, "you bring the best of what you do [. . .] and they bring the best of what they do to the table". Jay-Z describes himself as a student, learning from the beliefs, thoughts and experiences of those he collaborates with.

As you will see throughout this book, there's a curiosity beyond what's right in front of you that seems to be a hallmark of Outpacer success. Jay-Z's collaboration with artists from other musical genres has led to new music that can definitely be described as innovative – and with his record sales, his commercial success is in no doubt. But it's not just his musical genius that gets him to Outpacer status. In 2005 he laid down the prophetic lyric "I'm not a businessman, I'm a business, man". From starting record labels, restaurants and a clothing company to making major moves into sports management with Roc Nation Sports, and into the world of streaming with Tidal, Jay-Z's wide-reaching entrepreneurial efforts have been nothing short of brilliant. While clearly capable of going it alone, mostly he's looked to co-own or co-found new ideas, ventures and opportunities. Similarly, endorsements are based on long-term partnerships versus one-off deals.

Jay-Z's well calculated moves and deals in ventures he's passionate and knowledgeable about have ultimately proved to be a massive commercial success. In the world of rap, where it can be the "Big-I-am", he has looked to others for lessons and inspiration. He's taken that formula to the world of business and become a billionaire. The kid from one of the most deprived projects in America, who had to learn to hustle to survive, has collaborated and innovated in everything he's dedicated himself to. In doing so he's become an Outpacer of our time.

"People look at you strange, say you changed. Like you worked that hard to stay the same."

CHAPTER 5

DATA-DRIVEN INSIGHTS

What does that really mean?

Decision-makers rely on data-driven insights to set, improve, monitor and predict organizational performance and objectives. Experience and instinct are still valued, but must be informed, triangulated and reinforced through quality data, appropriate insights and smart analytics. Visualization tools and dashboards are cutting edge and user friendly. Data is properly managed and curated to ensure that users build and retain trust in the insights they receive. There is a total commitment to developing ethical artificial intelligence (AI) and using it in all decisions today and into the future.

Why is this important?

You can no longer run an organization based solely on emotion and experience. Today's Outpacers supplement every decision they make on real-time predictive data. In doing so, they are able to remove much of the bias and error that is inherent in human decision-making in order to make better investment and operational decisions.

So why have I decided to call this chapter Data-driven Insights? I could easily have gone with Artificial Intelligence (AI) and you would have got the point. AI is an exciting and relatively new field that is, or certainly should be, written in large on every CEO's to-do list. It can impact everything from data and processes to talent and risk management. So, in a sense, naming this chapter 'AI' might have seemed appropriate. But AI in isolation is not the exciting part. I'd like to focus on the outcomes, the insights that are generated by AI or good machine learning. We're talking about the importance of generating data-driven insights, so that your business is better able to predict where it needs to be in the future and get there before your customers even know where it is, and before your competitors can figure it out.

Where are we now?

Every company is talking about AI, and most have an AI experiment or pilot going on in their business, but we are still relatively early on in the evolution of how data is captured and used.

Gartner have a great model that explains the progression through the use of analytics:

Descriptive analytics, typically the starting point that's been around for a while, shows what has happened in the past. For example, a product manager can review user take-up across their target segments.

Diagnostic analytics explains why a certain event might have happened. So, the product manager can look at certain demographics and behaviors within the target user group and explain why take-up was higher in some demographics than others.

Predictive analytics uses the understanding from diagnostics to help predict what might happen in the future. Now it's getting a bit more interesting and helpful for our product manager because they can learn about and anticipate the take-up of certain demographics within the target user group – before it happens.

Prescriptive analytics anticipates what might happen when and suggests what should be done to make it happen. This is the kind of data-driven insight Outpacers use today and are perfecting for tomorrow. It gives an insight to our product manager that on their own they would not be capable of discovering. An insight that tells them if they do X, Y is highly likely to happen. And when Y is using your product, that becomes an extremely valuable insight.

Most companies are at very best to be found somewhere between descriptive and diagnostic analytics. They are possibly experimenting with predictive analytics, but discovering that it is a big step up. While most companies can comfortably say that they can gather data on customer behavior, it's a different matter to be able to analyze it effectively and use it to predict future outcomes.

Prescriptive analytics is a step up again and highly complex. According to Gartner, less than 3 per cent of companies are using it in their business. No surprise then, that this is where you'll find the Outpacers.

Today's Outpacers are moving beyond insights and into foresight, motivated by the ability to influence and change behavior (which opens up the huge topic of ethical AI, which we will talk about later). As a result of their data-driven focus, they're getting real, tangible benefits. They are able to make better decisions based on insights that had previously not been discovered. They can improve their service to the customer by delivering a better and more relevant offering. Online users can be served more relevant ads, and be recommended content or products that they already want or, better still, that they didn't know they wanted, but actually do!

This has freed up individuals' time. Spending countless manual hours on tasks like product cross-sell, which in some cases may not even have got to the right answer, is a thing of the past. Outpacers use AI to get instantaneous machine-led insights. This capacity release gives time back to key individuals who can then deliver further value with the time they have gained. As you'll see in Chapter 7 on Financial Excellence, I don't subscribe to the view that capacity release is simply another term for employee release. In an Outpacer, the value of an employee isn't just down to the role they perform, but also their understanding of the organization and personal commitment to the mVision. They are motivated people. If one element of their job is now done by a machine, it means that they have more time to work with the data-driven insights to add even more value to the organization.

Put your cape on!

With data-driven insights, it's almost as if your devoted talent have been given superhuman business powers, leaving mere mortals trailing in their wake. They can see through walls, around corners and into the future. And all that at lightning pace, allowing them to fly past the competition.

You can make a normal person very superhuman if you give them incredible data-driven insights. Twenty years ago, businesses would rely on extremely talented individuals who would use their experience and intelligence to look at a situation and advise the business on what to do next. Now that advice can come from a far greater field of people – and will be better. Let me demonstrate with an example from McLaren Applied, which used its experience of optimizing performance in the Formula 1 racing context to help air traffic controllers at Heathrow Airport.

Air traffic controllers sit in a highly complex data environment, with many planes approaching from multiple destinations, travelling at different speeds, with different winds, coming into different landing spots. It is a scenario in constant flux and often leads to incoming flights spending on average 20 minutes in a holding pattern over the airport. The controllers' ultimate priority is obviously to land each plane safely but the team's aim is also to prevent planes circling over the airport, which wastes fuel and often accounts for as much as 30 per cent of the airport's CO_2 emissions. By using sophisticated computer modelling, first developed to help Formula 1 drivers win, they can now advise each pilot on the best approach pattern, taking into account all the variations, thereby providing the optimal solution – a landing often without the need to circle.

Each air traffic controller, who is clearly already highly skilled, attains superhero status as they now have a unique insight into the best action to take next, which no human could have possibly computed in their head.

Don't wait for the tsunami

While many organizations are struggling to get an AI pilot to work, Outpacers are already looking beyond at how quantum computing will change everything we know, including perhaps the foundations of tech as we know it today.

At some point over the next decade we're likely to see the first implementation of quantum computing. We'll be witness to the kind of change in technology capability that we have never seen before, despite the pace of our current advances. Quantum computing will bring a leap that is almost unfathomable, as it manages to tackle challenges with overwhelming numbers of potentials and variables, beyond current computers' capability and certainly beyond that of the human mind. Its impact will be incredible, and will be felt across all industries, especially in areas like cybersecurity and AI. Outpacers are already thinking about simulating its impact on the things they do. While real implementations are still many years away, the fact that they're modelling it and preparing for it means that when the capability arrives, they will be ready for it.

Ten years plus might seem like a long way off, but it's a question of keeping pace. Fail to master today's environment and you'll struggle to move on to what comes next. You can be forgiven for feeling lost in the complexities of how quantum works or what it will do. The important point to grasp is that if you aren't mastering the ability to process data in today's environment, which in the future will be likened to watching TV in black and white, you will never reach a color future. In other words, there's no point in worrying about running if you haven't yet learnt to walk.

If quantum still feels other-worldly, think of the data explosion happening right now. A flood of new data is available every day from new systems and technologies. 5G, for example, is enabling significant increases in the capacity of Internet of Things networks and sensors, to such an extent that organizations are already struggling to process what they have, let alone the new data becoming available. It's a similar story with ERP (Enterprise Resource Planning) systems covering broad operational end-to-end processes across finance, HR, distribution and the supply chain, among others. Moving these processes from the basement (and on site) to the cloud creates monumental leaps in systems integration, data collection and the availability of much of the data that an enterprise is capturing. These new technologies are throwing up much more data than was previously the case.

I call this need to get on top of data and start using it properly "the data imperative". It's a bit like learning a new language: the longer you leave it, the harder it gets! Capisce?

But as we're outpacing, we're not interested in catching up or keeping up. We're talking about pushing for an advantage. Those who are bravest at pushing and experimenting will get the biggest leg-up as the technology starts to mature.

It's no coincidence that the biggest beneficiaries of the lockdowns during Covid-19 were the big tech giants who have been investing in digital and AI for years. When companies were forced to send employees to work from home and customers increasingly communicated with businesses online, it was the big tech giants who were able to capitalize on insights drawn from those widening digital footprints. There's no doubt that the investments they had made in their data models had a big part to play in their ability not just to cope, but to outpace.

Getting off the blocks

The starting point towards capturing data-driven insights is often automation of a set of processes. When these processes are completed by machines rather than humans, they produce previously unseen data insights.

Take this example: an organization has a number of suppliers that in turn lead to many complex supply chain contracts. Through weeks of hard graft, talented employees can spend valuable time trawling through each and every one to unearth the ways procurement teams have previously negotiated contracts, where any anomalies lie, where the most favorable terms can be found, and where any discounts should be applied across all supply contracts. With automation, the contracts can be read by a machine that will look across all the terms and provide positive insight in a fast, efficient way, saving countless hours and manpower.

There's a general understanding, certainly among wannabe Outpacers, of the benefits of taking manual processes and letting bots do the work. And automation is a great place to start on the journey to data-driven insights. In fact it's a key stepping stone. But it's a mistake to come at it from a pure cost perspective, simply focusing on having the bot replicate the manual task, believing that it can do the work of five people. Operational efficiency is clearly of benefit but it's just a foundation for the better products and services that can be delivered to customers from greater data insights. Outpacers ask what other things can we find out over and above what we knew before and how that will enhance what was done previously.

Don't let any automation slip through the net without taking the insights from the data. If you fail to find new insights, then you may not be looking hard enough. Think about the ton of data that new automation is producing and continue to analyze it with your teams to see if it provides greater insights into how to enhance that part of your organization.

Finding the gold nugget is a combination of great talent and great application of data-driven insights. It's not exactly finding the needle in the haystack or being a part of the great gold rush but it's not far off. You have to search for it, and do so skillfully, or it will pass you by. And once it's found, you must action it. A data-driven insight has no benefit until a human intervenes and acts upon it. Outpacers are constantly looking at automated processes, taking newly unearthed insights and then pushing on to reap the benefit.

Cr*p in, cr*p out

If the data that you put into your models isn't very good, or even worse is incorrect (and often that's the case), then the results will be equally poor and there'll be no chance of you predicting and influencing the future behavior of your customers. Not only is this disappointing from a results standpoint, but it also reduces the ability of the model to "learn", further compounding the challenge.

It's a very real problem. More than 60 per cent of executives cite a lack of quality data as a significant barrier to value creation. If you're not sure of the quality of the data going into your models or algorithms, there's no way you can trust what comes out.

The data flow may be substandard for a number of reasons. It may be incomplete, meaning that assumptions are made based on insufficient data, or anomalies creep in that throw it off kilter. For example, you buy a present online for a friend; it's perfect for them, but you have no interest in it at all. That action may corrupt the customer profile that online retailer holds on you, with the company believing it was a personal choice for you. If this anomaly is not accounted for, your preferences will be inadvertently and incorrectly recorded. Take this example to its conclusion: somewhere in the retailer a product manager is told that you are the ideal purchaser of the product, so money is spent promoting it to you, which unfortunately is a waste of time. Had the company added a tick-box to say it was a gift, or offered to wrap it, they may have avoided an inaccurate data profile and subsequent "data-driven mishap"!

It's not rocket science. The better the data you put in, the better the outcome. It's vitally important to get it right, and that means data must be treated with the seriousness it deserves. It's not a quick fix but an ongoing activity that stretches beyond the data team. Everyone who has a part to play with data input (see below) has a similar responsibility to ensure quality.

It's all connected

We've established the importance of data-driven insights, so why would you starve any one part of your organization of the results that can be achieved?

There's no doubt that focus should be on the front office, but unless it's seamlessly connected to the back office it cannot perform to its maximum potential. There needs to be good flow across the organization, avoiding data being siloed. The product manager might say that they want to reduce pricing on a product, believing that the price reduction will lead to an increase in users. That decision and action cannot be taken in isolation. It has to run from front to back in order that finance can understand the implications of it, the strategy can be understood and the data around the targeted customer group can be shared from the back to the front of the business.

Not only must there be a smooth flow, but data science and AI also have to be fully integrated into the fabric of the business. They can't sit with a standalone team that is expected to deliver breath-taking insights at the drop of a hat. CEOs should be thinking about how they can create a roadmap for data and analytics that enables integration and enterprise-wide thinking.

The reality today is that many organizations suffer from "cobblers' shoes", who may be good at offering their customers data-driven insights, but they struggle to give everyone in their own business, particularly those in the back office, the kind of data insights they really need. To truly outpace, you need to have that degree of focus and success in both the front office and back office. At KPMG achieving this is the work of an entire global practice called "connected", which encompasses everything an organization needs to connect the front office with the back office and all the parts in between.

Not only will a connected organization reap benefits in terms of enhanced product or service offerings, but it will also allow the front office to achieve the same kind of insights on its own people as it does on its customers. There's clearly value in foresight on your customers or users, but the ideal is to be able to get that same kind of foresight on talent, for example in retention, promotion and training, or how you spend your capital and what returns you'll get.

Imagine the power in being able to predict early on in someone's career that they are going to become a member of the C-Suite. That would allow you to put the requisite investment into the early part of their career, rather than relying on intuition as we do today. The ability to predict that talent trajectory would be a goldmine. We see a lot of predictive analytics and data insights being applied to sports in order to predict outcomes. Bookies use analytics to predict the outcome of a match. And anyone who's watched the film *Moneyball* will know the story behind Oakland Athletics' march to the playoffs on a shoestring budget, thanks to the statistics used to find talented but undervalued baseball players. Time has not stood still and scouts now use automated video analysis and tracking data before making multi-million-dollar investments in players. We have yet to see that kind of technology applied to business people and their talent trajectory, but it's coming. The Outpacers are already looking at talent models that enable them to better predict an individual's impact on a business and ability to perform at the highest levels.

"Mo money mo data insights"

As with everything in life, the more you put in, the more you get out. Outpacers are investing more and getting more insights and benefits as a result. You might say that's easy if you're worth a trillion dollars, that investing in new experimental areas is no risk and high reward. But even if you're not worth trillions, the question to ask is whether you are investing disproportionally to get results better than your competitors'.

I may have slightly overdone the car analogies (if you don't like them, I'm sorry, this probably won't be the last), but with data often described as the new oil, it would seem a shame not to use the analogy of data as fuel going into the car – you'll get significantly better performance the higher the quality of fuel. It makes everything perform better, faster, more smoothly and efficiently.

Organizations investing more in emerging technologies are also more likely to say they've already seen tangible value from their investment. A KPMG survey of executives at Global 2000 enterprises showed that while 18 per cent were already seeing tangible value from their AI investments, that number more than doubled, to 38 per cent, for those who invested more.

The human touch

Making the most of data-driven insights requires talent that has the insight and experience to know and understand the business, and the engineering expertise to program and continuously improve the models.

There needs to be a core data engineer capability of the highest standing. There's no doubt that there is a massive shortage of these skills, in what is a relatively new field. It's not impossible but it is difficult to secure the talent required. Having a team already devoted to a compelling mVision will undoubtedly help. The more purposeful and driven an organization, the more principled and focused, the more likely it is to attract the very best talent.

While securing new talent might be challenging, the very bright people you should already have within your organization can be upskilled, through a combination of training and opportunity to work on projects or pilots. One of the biggest challenges they face is the cultural change required to process and use data-driven insights in the right way. Executives used to going on an experienced hunch now need data evidence before proceeding to a decision. On the flip side, inexperienced individuals may use data to make a decision without the experience to know that the "recommended decision" isn't the right one and that it should be challenged. It's very important for individuals to know when the model is providing an insight that quite frankly isn't correct.

Think about technology giving your people new tools. Right back to Neolithic caveman times, humans have used tools to progress. Every industrial revolution has put more tools in the hands of humans to make them faster, better and more effective, and each time the new tools have initially been met with a lack of trust. Our current stage of development is the fourth industrial revolution and these data-driven insights and recommendations are tools that people need to get comfortable with to allow them to perform better.

Transparency is a huge help. There's a big difference between just being told to invest a million dollars here and being able to see why. For example, it's much better if you can say, "There is 86 per cent certainty that if we invest here, we will make 5x return based on the following data inputs." That transparency as to how a machine has reached a recommendation allows trust to be built. This will obviously be down to trial and error, particularly in the earlier stages. The more a machine advises a certain course of action and makes the correct call, the more you will trust it. The sooner AI becomes explainable, transparent and, most importantly, trusted, the sooner it will be accepted and productive.

The other big help is offering reassurance that machines' ability to recommend better decisions and insights will not render humans obsolete. Some jobs will disappear, but as we've seen throughout history, revolutionary advancements ultimately create more work and prosperity. I believe we will see the same here. Humans should be doing the tasks only humans can do. It is humans who will be making the ultimate decisions, but they must be talented enough to know how to interpret the data.

In a rapidly evolving field, there will always be new things to learn and stay on top of. This means that every organization forever more will need to continually raise its data IQ. And that includes every person within the organization, not just the engineer creating the algorithm or the person analyzing what comes out of it. It might not be your product manager's job to create the algorithm, but it is their job to make the right call based on the insight they've seen. The higher the data IQ they have, the more they will be able to contribute to improving the algorithm. They know the product better than anyone and their ability to contribute towards data inputs should be invaluable. Yes, you need a data team, but if everyone thinks it's that team's job alone, the insights are likely to be less reliable and people will trust them less.

In these early days of AI evolution there's no perfect playbook.

The bottom line is that you need top talent – motivated people with the intellectual curiosity to continually extend their own boundaries – to maximize the opportunity.

There's nothing artificial about the importance of trust and ethics

AI has the power to profoundly change how work gets done and decisions get made, but it needs to be deployed responsibly. I would highlight three areas of particular concern.

UNCONSCIOUS BIAS

Engineers can create algorithms that will determine where customers search on the internet, the news and stories they see and the products that are recommended to them. This gives a great deal of power to the engineers, who can influence and/or change people's behavior. If you don't have a diverse pool of people building the algorithms, it's very hard to avoid unconscious bias, and for these recommendations not to end up being skewed in a certain direction. There's no suggestion of these engineers trying to create bias, but they can only act on their own experience. As I've already highlighted, there's a shortage of bright, capable data scientists, and at the moment it's more than likely that the talent pool is centered around male graduates from highly sought-after US colleges and universities, who tend to have a similar background.

Because of the importance of data science and algorithms specifically, if there is an implicit problem with what's coming out, it's important to acknowledge it. Data integrity is crucial to your success as a team, but any scientist will tell you that if an experiment has a set of data that is not pure, the result won't count. Data science is a science. As with any other form of science, if there is a bias within it and it is acknowledged, then work towards solving the problem can begin.

It's difficult to prove unconscious bias at this early stage, but you can look at your team and decide whether it represents the customer base you're serving. It's highly likely that you will not have a match. If that's the case, acknowledge it and try to build a solution with the same kind of rigor that you would show if you knew the data set was poor. A first step might be to divert training, coaching and mentoring support into your organization to help people who perhaps didn't have the opportunity to study data science at college.

PRIVACY AND SECURITY

There is far greater clarity now from governing bodies and regulators around the world to ensure that organizations collecting data have a clear set of rules as to what they can and cannot do. That hasn't always been the case. That clarity allows organizations to ensure they are compliant. Whether or not they like these rules, there is an undeniable trust factor that comes into play for Outpacers. Their future trajectory and growth will be dependent on them being trusted by their customers and users, who, thanks to regulatory interventions, have a greater say in organizations' activities. The right to be forgotten under the General Data Protection Regulations (GDPR), under which an EU citizen has the right to demand an organization erase their personal data, forms part of a growing trend. If you breach the rules or are fined for not taking them seriously, customers and users will find a way to show their displeasure.

This is too important an area for it to be solely the responsibility of the governance team. Privacy must be part of everyone's job, not just one department. Everyone must understand that it's a reflection of the quality of the work they do and the trust they share with their customers. It shouldn't be hard. Everyone within an organization is a customer themselves and should fully appreciate that selling their beliefs and behaviors to another organization without their permission doesn't reflect the values of a good person or business. In the (hopefully unlikely) event that there are still a few individuals who are not on board, transparency across the business can help with calling out poor behavior and rooting out individuals who are not living the values within the mVision framework.

ACCOUNTABILITY

One of the topics of greatest concern to governments, regulators and consumers is the potential power of AI in the hands of a small number of large organizations. One of the biggest drivers of that is a lack of understanding about where AI is going.

In all industrial revolutions there has been fear about the impact of new advancements and technology. While there clearly are some areas of concern for society and governments around the power of AI, the best way to mitigate this is for organizations with advanced capability – no matter what their size – to be open and transparent about their goals and objectives and the way they are governing themselves. If you put everyone in a basement with hoods on and refuse to engage with the outside world, people will worry about what you are up to. If, however, you can demonstrate that AI will be used within a framework that has a positive impact on the world, and that follows the principles and values set out in your mVision, you will inspire stakeholders within and outside the organization rather than feed concern.

The race has started . . . Have you?

Many companies are already overwhelmed with the data they have. The reality is that today's data quantities will feel like a data lake compared to the data ocean that's coming. There are plenty who will tell you, correctly, that if you can't swim in the lake, you'll drown in the ocean. I prefer a more "glass half full" take on the situation. This is a complex new field to learn, much like learning a new language and culture. It doesn't happen overnight and given that there's no set playbook, there will undoubtedly be a few missteps. But the sooner you embrace the change and get going with big investment, the sooner you'll start enjoying the results.

ANNE WOJCICKI

Some years ago, I was at a conference in California and excited to hear from the next speaker, Anne Wojcicki, CEO of personal genomics and biotechnology company 23andMe. It was a small but senior audience, a pretty intimate fireside chat. While we were waiting for it to start, I asked the lady next to me if she knew much about 23andMe. "Not much," she replied, then pointed at Wojcicki. "Just that this woman probably saved my life."

Wow! In a day of speakers covering topics from the privacy controls at Facebook to Verizon rolling out 5G connectivity, I wasn't prepared for something so personal.

The woman explained that as a result of her 23andMe test results, she had sadly discovered she was at high risk of developing cancer. As a young, healthy and very busy individual, getting cancer wasn't exactly on her radar. Following the 23andMe results, she went to the doctor the next day and was ultimately able to avert a situation that could have become fatal.

As I listened to Wojcicki talk about her business, I was overcome with admiration for someone so passionate about her mission, taking incredibly personal data and providing critical health insights that can save lives. I sat and thought, *It's going to be hard going to sleep tonight feeling I'm doing anything worthwhile by comparison.*

23andMe was established in 2006 by Wojcicki and co-founders Linda Avey and Paul Cusenza. They have a mission to revolutionize healthcare (specifically: "to help people access, understand and benefit from the human genome"). They have two goals: to empower consumers by giving them greater access to their own health information, and to amass an unprecedented stockpile of genetic information about as much of the world's population as possible.

Wojcicki's lightbulb moment came while having dinner with a scientist who was working on a genetics project. She asked him, "If you had the world's data – if every single person in the world was sequenced, and you had their medical records – would you be able to solve most healthcare problems?" He answered with an unequivocal yes, and with that she was set on gathering that data and using it to benefit those who supplied it.

In this chapter we've talked about turning talented and skilled people into superheroes, by providing data-driven insights that transform what they can do. By giving the already extraordinary humans working in healthcare insights from data that can help prevent illness or fast-track treatment, we really can empower them to put their capes on and change the course of someone's life.

As with any emerging field, there are always challenges. Data privacy and regulatory approvals in relation to the healthcare sector continue to require a high level of focus. I put both firmly in the earlier section on trust and ethics. You need a large data set to create the insights that drive the value, but that is only possible if people trust you enough to hand over their DNA. And from an ethical standpoint, how you share sensitive health information with someone is incredibly important.

Wojcicki believes: "Big data is going to make us all healthier. [. . .] Genetics is part of an entire path for how you're going to live a healthier life . . . Everyone's going to die and everyone's going to get sick at some point. But I do believe that there are choices you can make in life that will make you as healthy as possible."

With the world still reeling from the effects of the Covid-19 pandemic, health has never been more in the spotlight. I passionately believe that data-driven insights in healthcare will move us from focusing on treatment to focusing on prevention of illness. For that to happen we will be reliant upon people like Wojcicki and her team making bold and courageous steps to harness the power of data-driven insights, allowing us all to live better and healthier lives.

If that doesn't sound like an Outpacer, I don't know what does!

SIR LEWIS HAMILTON

Sir Lewis Hamilton is the seven-time Formula 1 world champion, and an Outpacer icon on and off the track. His driving talent is indisputable but data-driven insights have been a major contributor to his incredible success, a fact he's more than happy to share. As he says, "I don't drive by the seat of my pants and happen to win races. I work very hard to interpret the data and drive a certain way."

Sir Lewis started in go-karts aged eight, keenly supported by his father Anthony, who would analyze his son's competitors, specifically when they would brake ahead of a corner. He would then mark a point much closer to the corner (allowing much later braking) to get his son an advantage. There may have been no advanced algorithm, but from the very start of his career, Sir Lewis trusted insights that could help him win.

F1 was an early adopter of data-driven insights for several reasons. Firstly, it works. When the margin between winning and losing can be hundredths of a second, data really can make the difference. Secondly, it's an engineering-led industry. It's in everyone's DNA to be open to what an engineer can do to improve performance. Finally, many big tech companies sponsor the F1 teams. These firms give F1 teams access to emerging data and analytics tools, machine learning and AI in order that they can both test it in an incredible high-data environment and showcase its benefits in an exciting way.

Meshing those data-driven insights with talented individuals who will perform better as a result is as important as creating the insights themselves. I call it the human touch. Sir Lewis talks about "all the data the engineers are studying and analyzing", saying, "My job is not only to drive, but to bring the human factor to it – always challenging them – to get that balance of experience and data." And that's true for any organization wanting to use data-driven insights to get ahead.

You need to bring data insights, mesh them with human experience and extract an insight not previously possible. Sir Lewis gives the example of being told by his data engineers during a race in Abu Dhabi that he didn't need to pit and that his current tires could finish the race. However Lewis was concerned that, while not pitting would guarantee the win, a blow-out of his tires would mean race over. Despite his skepticism, he trusted the data and got the win.

Sir Lewis is not only driven by a desire to succeed but also by the need to push diversity and inclusiveness. This has been deep-rooted since his days of being "the only Black kid at the [go-kart] track" and now he is still the only Black driver to ever race in F1.

Following the murder of George Floyd, he lambasted F1 and other drivers for not doing enough to support an anti-racism message and the Black Lives Matter movement. He persuaded the Mercedes F1 team – forever known as the Silver Arrows – to change their livery for the first time in history to black. On winning his seventh world championship he said, "This year I've been driven not just by my desire to win on the track, but by a desire to help push our sport and our world to become more diverse and inclusive. [. . .] I will continue to push for equality within our sport, and within the greater world we live in." He set up the Hamilton Commission with the Royal Academy of Engineering, to help engage more Black young people with science, technology, engineering and mathematics.

Sir Lewis is undoubtedly an Outpacer posterchild for data-driven insights. But he is equally committed to using his F1 platform to drive greater change in the world. As you reflect on what it takes to be an Outpacer, know this: being brilliant at one thing isn't enough. Outpacers are the full package and they never stop wanting to impact both in their chosen field and for the greater good.

CHAPTER 6

AGILE TECHNOLOGY

What does that really mean?

The organization views their technology assets and capabilities as a differentiator. The technology estate is designed to enable agility and flexibility for the business, while providing access to actionable data insights through common data platforms. The organization adopts the right technologies at the right time and in the right parts of the business to remove barriers, increase speed, improve capacity, scale up ideas and create opportunities for the business to succeed in the market. It requires a cloud-based approach that scales with the business and provides colleagues with the tools they need to succeed, while delighting customers with an omni-channel approach that delivers an exceptional digital customer experience.

Why is this important?

World-class technology performance that delivers real technology agility is critical to providing the business with what it needs to outpace the market. By focusing on creating a more agile technology estate, Outpacers drive improved efficiency and effectiveness and give the business the ability not just to keep up with customers and competitors, but to get ahead, creating an unassailable lead for the organization. It raises the overall tech IQ of the business and ensures that everyone is willing and able to use the very latest digital tools to make them the very best they can be.

The legacy challenge

- "Another !@#$%?! outage! I just want it to work!" CEO
- "We've just had throw more money at Bob to stop him retiring. He's the only one who knows that platform." Senior IT Manager
- "If we don't change the pricing on these products pronto, we're going to be in deep you know what, but IT are saying it'll take six weeks!" Product Manager
- "The ERP system can only report the numbers by product line. I can't see it by country, so I don't even know if we're profitable in all the countries we're in." Head of Finance
- "The new regulations say we've got to permanently erase all that customer data within that timeframe, but we don't even know if that's possible." Compliance Manager
- "So . . . do we just have to pay the ransom?" Chair of the Board
- "I'm all about the customer, boss, but our CRM is garbage. Mrs Jones just complained again, swore off our services forever and did a massive rant online because we've mailed her dead husband again! Honestly, I don't blame her!" Head of Customer Operations

Any of those comments sound familiar? There are many great organizations with ambitious and talented people, a great strategy, loyal customers and cash in the bank . . . yet they're not outpacing. Why? One of the most prevalent derailers is those organizations' technology estate. There are multiple reasons, excuses, well thought-through logic and ways to articulate the situation, but the simple fact is that the poor tech capability is like a noose around the organization's neck, so you hear things like the above.

For the shiny new tech companies, you'll be laughing at all this, saying, "I'm in the cloud – this doesn't apply to me." And to some extent that's true. Much of the above relates to companies that have been around for years and have legacy tech estates creating multiple problems. If any of it sounds familiar, things need to change. Fast. For those of you chuckling at their misfortune, don't laugh too hard. Once again, you need to remind yourself that the only constant is change, so how you work to ensure you have agile technology and can stay ahead is key for you.

Across all industries, there are examples of organizations that have a strong desire to be great but are hampered by unreliable systems that frequently have problems, because someone has decided that the old legacy systems can't be replaced just yet. Unfortunately it's just flogging a dead horse. In these businesses, systems and applications don't talk to each other, and for all the advances in AI, it's impossible to access the data because it's all over the place. It's frustrating for everyone and the worrying thing is that some in the organization have stopped complaining and started to accept things the way they are. Disaster. We've all had that moment when the tech is dead. We've probably all had that moment when it's not the first time and you're at the end of your tether. Its failure is eroding your trust, so you just go back to the way you used to do it. Outpacers don't go backwards!

Ultimately the lack of capability is undermining business

performance, masking key information and data required to run the business, exposing the organization to significant increases in risk, compliance, regulatory requirements and cyber attacks, and finally impeding the product team's ability to delight customers.

Often the key factor is cost. But as time ticks by, so do the maintenance bills. It's time to stop the bleeding, as what was once a cut with a plaster is now an artery that needs urgent attention before the situation becomes terminal.

Outpacers do not find themselves in these situations. They know that technology agility is critical to providing business flexibility and responsiveness to market opportunity. By focusing on creating a more agile technology estate, they create value for the business and the end customers.

Think about the technology estate in the context of humans using tools to advance themselves. Every industrial revolution has brought new tools to humanity, further advancing life on Earth for humankind. Your technology estate is an incredible toolbox that has the kit you need to operate and to outpace in the fourth industrial revolution. While it's a simple analogy, it's less straightforward to make it happen. It's not just about cloud strategy, data strategy, AI capability or cyber. It's about having the very best tools in the hands of the right people (your people and your customers) at the right time. When you get it right, your technology estate provides the tools each individual needs to succeed and ultimately what the business needs to outpace the market!

In my view, every company is now a tech company, so understanding how to be great at tech is an absolute imperative for every business. To be an Outpacer, you need to ensure that your company has a very high tech IQ, and that means that everyone has a role to play.

Agile technology as a competitive advantage

In order to gain a competitive advantage, you really need to nail the "agile" in agile technology. It's worth digging into what I mean by the word "agile". It's a well-known adjective that is used to describe an ability to move quickly and easily. For an Outpacer, movement is key: you never stand still because the market, and crucially your customers, are constantly moving and changing. Your ability to move in the digital economy is going to be dependent on your technology, and that will determine whether you are an Outpacer.

But agility is also a methodology that goes beyond technology. The agile way of working is a way for organizations to react to change. It changes the way an entire organization operates, transforming hierarchical departments into small self-steering teams consisting of members with different backgrounds – for example, from marketing, sales, customer experience, admin, data and tech. It helps organizations to get a better understanding of changing customer needs, to quickly and continuously improve customer interaction and to implement smarter and, in most cases, more efficient ways of working. While increasing transparency, it breaks down internal silos and often creates a happier company culture, leading to increased employee satisfaction.

So when I talk about "Agile Technology" I'm really using the term agile blending both definitions, because to be an Outpacer you need to embed the principles of agile within your organization while adopting and deploying the right technology that will allow you to change quickly and easily. The goal is not to become more agile than you were before, but to become more agile than everyone (and at the very least your competition). And that means being honest with yourself about the technology you have available to your devoted talent. If it is not delivering a real competitive advantage for them, it needs to be changed.

Enabling tech (for humans!)

With every company being a tech company, understanding how to be great at tech is an absolute imperative no matter which sector you sit in. Raising the tech IQ means that not only does everyone have a key tech role to play, but in order for them to play that role, they need to be introduced to the tech in a way that takes into account that they are a) human and b) likely to have to change their behavior. That is the only way for them and the organization to get full benefit from the new tech.

We talked earlier about the importance of thinking of technology as a set of tools that can get the very best out of your devoted talent. This helps you to remember that you've got to ensure the tools are going to be well received by the humans who need to adopt them! You have to develop the ability to properly inform your talent about the technology and motivate them to use it. If you had a leaking tap and someone handed you a wrench, that probably wouldn't be enough to ensure you could fix the tap! Don't just think of it as training. It's far more than that – you've got to ensure your devoted talent actually wants to use the tech, and the best way to achieve that is to hand them new tools that show you've listened and understood what help they need to perform at their optimum level.

In an Outpacer there's a constant two-way dialogue between those responsible for the tech and those working across the business. The technology that underpins the organization is the technology that everyone needs, because there is a deep understanding of how the business operates and what it needs from technology to drive it better and faster towards the mVision. It's the right tools, in the right hands, at the right time and, importantly, with the comms, training and support to ensure that the devoted talent wants and loves to use the enabling tech that the business needs to Outpace.

A matter of survival

If you are facing the reality of a legacy technology estate that isn't necessarily falling apart, but certainly couldn't be defined as agile, then you need to rethink and potentially rebuild everything. The point is that your tech estate doesn't have to be broken for tech transformation to be an imperative for your future survival.

You might feel that this is an overwhelming challenge, that it's too hard, too expensive and would take too long. But, as we've already covered, if you don't have an agile technology estate underpinning your business, you're undermining your organization to the point where you are slowly but surely removing the vital oxygen that it needs to survive. So don't feel overwhelmed. Take a deep breath and start to imagine your agile technology future. Remember that where there's a will, there's a way! Take Fox Corporation – they did it and should act as your inspiration.

Wind the clock back to 2019 for one of the biggest media deals of all time, when Disney paid $71.3 billion for some of the incredible film and TV assets held by 21st Century Fox. But not everything went in the deal. The Murdochs weren't done, and Fox Corp emerged with hefty ambitions for the future. Fox Corp was now a news and sports company, focused on the assets it had retained, which included Fox Sports, Fox News and the Fox TV network. With the huge cash pile from the Disney deal on hand, it had to be ready for future opportunities in the new digital era that the 2020s would hold.

Fox Corp might have been described as "new Fox", but in reality, it was no spring chicken and much of its technology had been built up over many years. So when CTO Paul Cheesbrough looked under the hood and thought about the digital race they were about to embark on, he concluded that the engine he saw wasn't good enough to ensure the win. It wasn't going to deliver the vision the Murdochs had for the new business. So the Fox Corp team set about building a new engine from scratch, one that would give them the necessary horsepower to outpace the competition.

They used the huge deal to create a moment of truth for the business, one where it was acknowledged that while the tech they had wasn't in any way crippling the business, it also wasn't going to secure their future. So rather than moving forward with the legacy estate, they used the moment to envision a new tech future for Fox Corp and imagine a tech estate that would give them everything they needed to succeed. There were plenty of competing priorities during the deal, so arguably it might have been easier to take a massive technology transformation off the to-do list. And it certainly wasn't without risk. It's not like they had time for a pit-stop to change the engine, as they couldn't exactly press pause on their 24/7 news channels or all their live sport! So, while they used the deal to recognize the need for change and to drive the transformation, they still did it during working hours. They didn't get a time-out. They just knew they had to get it done.

When it came to the engine rebuild, Fox went all out to create what I would describe as a truly agile technology estate. They eliminated all of their data centers and migrated to what they described as "an entirely elastic infrastructure". They went on to build a brand new 8K- and 5G-enabled video distribution and streaming facility, in partnership with Amazon Web Services and Arizona State University. They consolidated disparate enterprise systems and teams into a single, modern, best-of-breed cloud stack overseen by a single operations team. They further enhanced their approach to cyber security, based upon a zero-trust architecture. This incredible new engine would require some special driving talent, so they chose to combine the existing and experienced team with some new drivers, scaling their software engineering and product development skills. And they didn't sit back and marvel at their new toys. Instead they shifted their mindset to growth and enablement of the business.

Fox Corp not only used the deal with Disney to reimagine what they needed, they also used the two-year timeframe in which the deal had to be completed to put a deadline on the completion of the new technology architecture. They estimated they completed over five years of work within that two-year timeframe. And at the end of that journey, Cheesbrough was happy to report, "Significant efficiency was delivered into the core enterprise technology operation through modernization and consolidation. More importantly, the new capabilities delivered through this focus are bringing speed, agility and creative benefits to the company in a way that the old systems and practices just simply couldn't support."

What's more, they found that a legacy estate has a massive correlation with the culture, skills and focus of a team. As they walked away from their legacy estate it freed up the team to focus on what really mattered to them – building value and enabling and driving growth. Fox Corp also re-equipped its talent base, focusing on DE&I improvements and upskilling in software skills. They found walking away from legacy wasn't just a systems thing; it also gave them the chance for a fresh start.

It's a great story of what's possible when you're honest about what you've got, are clear on what you need and have the courage and conviction to get it done. At the time it may not feel like a matter of survival, but often it is.

How to do it?

FIND THE RIGHT LOVER AND AVOID THE HANDCUFFS

In a loving relationship you'll find give and take, with both individuals having the other person's best interests at heart. Neither one plans to screw over the other for their own benefit. That's the kind of relationship that all parties should be looking for in a commercial context, and in particular when it comes to people who are trusted with your most sensitive assets.

When you're looking to team up with tech suppliers, make sure that you know what you're getting into and you understand just what it is you want to get out of the relationship. One thing's for sure: big tech companies have very sophisticated and talented sales teams, so you need to ensure that you're buying what you actually need, not what you're being told you need. This really isn't a one-night stand. You're looking for the right life partner, so look past smooth operators to check what you're getting yourself into. Sometimes you have to swipe left . . .

Due to the enormous cost of IT and tech, many companies have traditionally entered into longer-term contracts to secure the lowest cost from their tech suppliers. But those contracts often act like handcuffs: while the costs may be lower, it inevitably means less flexibility. Long-term restrictive contracts can damage your agility, and for many organizations today, it's those contracts that are holding them back from making changes that they want to make. The handcuffs might have seemed fun at the time, but if you don't have the key, things can get uncomfortable very quickly.

In contrast, the cloud operators use utility-based pricing, providing flexibility that is much more attractive. You don't get saddled with tech that's out of date in your own environment. Instead you lock in to tech roadmaps set by the biggest and best in the business who provide you access to almost unlimited compute power and storage. It's a very attractive, low-risk way of managing your tech, providing you with access to experts who have the advantage of operating at scale.

When you decide that cloud is the way to go, make sure you pick an organization that you can truly partner with, because you're going to be very dependent on them, in sickness and in health! With technology there are always going to be challenges and problems, so the collective ability, willingness and cultural alignment between you and your tech partner are crucial to long-term success.

As you migrate critical data, applications and systems to the cloud, you need to ensure you retain tech talent within your business so that you stay in control of your technology future. You may not need the same size of team, but that talent is crucial to ensuring that the business is getting what it needs today and that your tech suppliers are working hard to ensure they have the tech capability you need for tomorrow. You can't have an imbalance in talent, where your supplier's tech knowledge surpasses that of your organization.

That's not to say that your entire infrastructure should sit with one cloud provider. You may have the bulk sitting with one, but you must always have enough leverage with another that you can pull them in if need be. A multi-provider strategy is a must.

Finally, you need to ensure that your tech partners love you and your mVision. Your tech suppliers should be as devoted to your organization as your own talent is. They should be thinking and designing tech roadmaps that enhance your whole business because they want you to be able to utilize their tech to make you better. Your tech partners are a vital component of your tech ecosystem and when you get that right, your agile technology capability gets a very big lift.

KNOW YOUR BOUNDARIES

I believe that moving to the cloud is a business imperative for everyone, but you have important choices to make about the type of cloud deployment you need. They each have a different boundary and you need to determine the best one for you. The three types of cloud are hybrid, public and private, with each offering different advantages in terms of scalability, flexibility, security and cost agility. Think of private as your own ringfenced environment with no common servers, a holiday apartment that no one else has access to but run by the resort management company. At the other end of the spectrum is the public cloud, where your room is in a shared Airbnb house that offers communal resources with greater flexibility and options to pay for other rooms if you need them.

You need to pick the right cloud environment to suit your needs. If you want to hire 100 employees next month or grow your customer base by 100,000, you've got to ensure you have enough compute and storage to handle the surge. Outpacers scale very quickly so an agile technology capability is key to ensuring that scaling at pace can be achieved (seemingly) effortlessly.

Outpacers are huge cloud users but they do so with a deep understanding of their boundaries. They are brilliant at choosing the right environment for them in relation to which application should sit where, who should have access and any associated risks. What you put in the cloud and on what terms is crucial to your performance and your overall agility. It's key to remember that if you move everything to the cloud, once it's gone, it's pretty much gone for good. You need to be very clear about the level of control and ownership you want and need, and when.

Public cloud is the most popular model of cloud computing and there's good reason for thinking that everything that can be moved to public should be. Private cloud arguably fails to bring the benefits of access to scale (in comparison to public), making it harder to adapt at pace. The counter-argument is that private allows segregation of your entire environment and therefore allays concerns companies may have about security or data leakage. For those still so reluctant to move sensitive applications or data to the cloud, remember hyper-scale cloud providers can maintain far greater safety and segregation of their environment than most can achieve in-house. With every organization now susceptible to cyber and ransom attacks, ask yourself who you would put your money on to best protect you – the people within an organization doing everything they can but without the resources to win the fight, or those who have to do this as their day job?

We've already talked a lot about data and analytics, their critical role and the fact that the imperative to use data is only going to increase. For me, this is one of your most important decisions. If data is the new oil, then think about getting to your data in the cloud as extracting oil from an oil field. It's very valuable and you need to get access to it easily, while ensuring those not welcome can't get in. So be clear on what's best for you and your business by setting the boundaries exactly where they need to be.

GET A GREAT CAPTAIN FOR YOUR TECH SHIP

The captain of your tech ship is a really important role. It doesn't matter whether this person is called Chief Technology Officer, Chief Information Officer or Chief Digital Officer (for this chapter we'll go with CTO). What does matter is that they possess incredible leadership skills and that they are an all-round business guru who can unlock the benefits of tech for the whole business and its customers.

As CTO one of their most important roles is to drive innovation and transformation in the business. They will need to have an overarching view of the enterprise architecture and the data strategy. But they will equally need to build on those elements with the people within the business who can drive that strategy forward. They need to see the opportunities that new technologies might bring and work out how that can be applied by people in a consistent, standardized way across the organization. In today's digital economy, arguably they also need to act like the chief strategist.

Their mission is to give their talented colleagues the tools to help them be better at their jobs. And not just give them the tools, but through brilliant comms and engagement, to ensure that they get used in an optimal way. There's a huge responsibility for change management and for navigating the company culture, understanding what will fly and what won't. Arguably, in today's digital economy, a board should take the same care in appointing the CTO as they do the CEO and CFO.

One of my observations of the non-Outpacer is that they often take a software application and ruin it by over-customizing it. The tech leader will often be inundated with requests for modifications, add-ons and changes. While there's definitely a balance to be struck, given that the tech needs to give you agility, the ability of the CTO to reduce customizations, using their business acumen and leadership skills to be a great judge of whether it's an absolute necessity, is crucial. Customizations often bring complexity in support and deployment. They are costly and take time for coding, testing and deployment. Selecting the software that works for the business in the first place and doesn't need a huge amount of customization is definitely a better way to go!

Leadership skills are also paramount when it comes to decision-making on when to adopt new technology. This can be contentious, so ultimately you need a wise and experienced leader to call it right. Sometimes it could be right to be a first mover, sometimes it's better to be a fast follower. Making the wrong call can have dire consequences, so the CTO needs to be decisive. As with the balance on customizations, not everyone is going to agree with their decision.

Clearly then, the CTO won't always be popular. Saying no to demanding colleagues is never easy, but it's easier with the right support and sponsorship from the board. That board support needs to be given if the captain is to have the authority and resources to navigate the choppy tech waters. Two-way trust is built through openness and transparency, leading to greater understanding and support from the board for investment. The tech leaders that fail are the ones celebrating the complexity of tech and its almost unparalleled use of jargon to make themselves seem like a master of some lost art. The opposite approach wins out every time. Keep it simple and take everyone with you.

When you think about how much money is spent on tech, it's perhaps obvious that two-way trust is also crucial between your CTO and your CFO. In the non-Outpacer that's not the case; there is mistrust and misunderstanding, which leads to indecision. In an Outpacer, tech partners with finance so they can work together to judge the worthiness of new tech investments. There is an understanding that, in order to be the best in the use of tech, there will be some projects that go great and some that don't. In the ones that don't, adopting a fail-fast environment, where there is a budgetary allowance for a margin of error for deployments that don't deliver and get cut off quickly, is a must. By working as another dynamic duo, the CTO and CFO help the business to see the bigger picture and make the right calls on new tech investments. Often time is crucial, so the ability of Tech and Finance to be agile in the way they work together will in turn have a significant bearing on the organization's ability to have an agile technology estate.

Under the leadership of the CTO, the whole tech team often operate like an invisible force making sure that everything is working as it should 24/7. In fact they are often the unsung heroes in an Outpacer. When the tech is working brilliantly no one comments (compliments that everything is working are hard to come by). When it goes wrong it's a different story. It's like kryptonite to all the superheroes doing their jobs. In today's digital age, they are literally left incapable of operating.

When things go wrong, you need a CTO with cool composure to gather the team and the tech partners to quickly get you back on course. Think of the captain standing at the helm of a fantastic yacht. You don't even notice they're there as you sail around in the sunshine, but when you encounter a massive storm threatening the lives of everyone on board, all the passengers immediately look to the captain to save the day. That's when talent, experience and a cool head count for everything. The passengers might be frustrated that their perfect sunshine has gone, but they also couldn't be any more grateful when you get them back safe and sound.

It's also pretty handy if your captain just happens to have served in the navy, because this individual is also your most important security guard, implementing both defensive and offensive strategies to deal with the threats that are coming your way all day, every day. Cyber threats are now at the top of the risk list for any organization, and the higher your profile, the greater a target you are. Cyber security now needs to be an organizational capability, with every member of the organization playing their part to keep the business safe. That capability standard needs to be set by the CTO, who has to have the right capability to keep everyone out of harm's way.

YOU GET WHAT YOU PAY FOR

When an NFL general manager said to talent agent Jerry Maguire in the eponymous film, "I can't afford that", Maguire's memorable response was "No one said winning is cheap." Much like the pay for professional athletes, the cost of tech can make you wince, but ultimately if you understand it's an organizational must, you figure out that it's worth it. And what's more, there really isn't a shortcut. As author Kurt Vonnegut wrote in *Cat's Cradle*, "In this world, you get what you pay for."

Unfortunately, buying and investing in tech isn't as simple as agreeing what is required and finalizing an amount to cover it. The tech budget needs some flex in it to cope with the unexpected, and the CTO's great relationship with finance comes into its own when the unthinkable happens. Let's take what would have seemed a pretty unrealistic, sci-fi scenario earlier this decade: there's a global pandemic meaning that all colleagues are forbidden to leave their homes and urgently need video comms capability at home. In addition, all retail outlets are to close, meaning that the organization will need to go 100 per cent digital if it is to survive. That sort of change isn't going to be cheap and there's no choice to be made. While some companies baulked at the eye-watering expenditure, the companies that thrived through Covid-19 were those who channeled investment into their tech.

Cutting corners is counterproductive. Back to the example above, skimping on the video comms infrastructure needed to keep colleagues engaged and collaborating might save some money in the short term. But those gains are quickly wiped out when the unreliable video interrupts meetings, reduces productivity and puts everyone in a bad mood.

Meanwhile, making the investment so that everything works has the opposite effect. I've visited many amazing tech locations, and the ones that had the cool tech and enhanced my experience as a visitor really stand out in my mind. They leave a positive and lasting impression that those organizations are investing and making sure everything is going to work. The McLaren Technology Centre is a great example. Designed to reflect the company's design and engineering expertise, it's like looking at a spaceship, and a bit like standing in one once you're inside. Every employee exudes pride and if you're me, you can't help but stand there in awe, thinking that all this tech is amazing and I really must put owning a McLaren on my bucket list!

So don't skimp on investing in tech. Be open and transparent on the business cases with the whole organization. For example, many organizations are drawn to the cloud, believing that there are significant cost savings to be had. And it's true that not having to pay for capital expenditure, but rather being charged for the computing on-demand could conceivably save you money. But it would be a massive mistake to think that the business case for cloud is around cost savings. Moving to the cloud massively enhances your tech capability and helps build an agile technology estate. That's about investing to better the whole organization, not about saving IT costs.

USE YOUR RADAR

Any good captain knows that they need a good radar. They need to have the very best tech insights giving them a clear view on what's happening today and what will happen in the future. Having a 360 degree view will ensure that you as an organization have the agility to change and adapt, and understand and prepare for the risks that could affect your business from a tech standpoint.

The mission is to provide your people with the best tools, so the CTO has got to know what's coming up on the horizon or lurking down below. If change is constant, your tech is out of date from the minute you deploy it. It is constantly changing and therefore your radar reflects that constant flux, where risk and opportunity come at you relentlessly. It's time to stand back from the day-to-day operations and ensure the CTO can see the bigger picture on behalf of the whole organization.

Most CEOs and boards will say that they can handle difficult situations, but what they want to avoid is surprises. By using their version of the radar, the tech team can see the signals of change and be proactive, prepared and organized around the risks and opportunities that tech can offer the business. That in turn allows the organization to be prepared from a budget, implementation, change and transformation standpoint.

Horizon scanning is an imperative to help with the selection of innovative tech at the best time for the organization – not too late, not too early. Outpacers approach it with discipline, piloting and trialing new tech quickly and cheaply with users who give real-time feedback, so they can determine whether to employ it more broadly. In an Outpacer everyone is open to trialing new tools, knowing that the goal is to provide everyone with the best kit to do their jobs. And that takes us back to the tech IQ of the organization. The better the tech in the organization, the higher the IQ and the higher the agility. The radar ensures nothing gets missed, with threats and opportunities constantly evaluated to ensure the tech capability and the tools provided to the business are the very best available.

Conclusion

To be an Outpacer, think of agile technology as being like the body of your favorite athlete. I'm sure whoever you're picturing is extremely fit, combining great strength, skills and agility to move fast when the moment comes. This athlete works on that physical prowess all the time, investing time and energy into their training in order to be the best. They never stand still and are always looking for an edge to get ahead of the competition. When they are playing their chosen sport, their brain knows what to do and their body responds in perfect harmony with whatever is required to win.

In an Outpacer, the organization is like the brain and the technology capability is like the body of an athlete. Unlike competitors, whose brain says one thing but the body is unable to respond, in the Outpacer the agile technology springs into action, driving the whole business forward in total harmony.

When you think of a six-pack for the tech team in an average organization, you're probably thinking about their beer intake! Say six-pack in the context of a tech team at an Outpacer and it should conjure up images of some finely tuned abs to remind you of the incredible agility that sits within the organization and is ready to win when the moment comes.

THOMAS KURIAN

Thomas Kurian lives and breathes using agile technology to create a competitive advantage. As CEO of Google Cloud, he has not only been transforming his own business with huge success, but also building a cloud offering that optimizes and delivers on the agile technology characteristic, battling Amazon Web Services and Microsoft Azure to put Google Cloud Platform (GCP) right in the middle of what was previously a two-horse race.

While some talk about the cloud market as if it's mature, I believe that for GCP it's still pretty early days. Despite being a business that had world-leading engineering and technical prowess, it had previously been unable to gain traction with enterprise customers at the scale of its two larger rivals. The company faced two main challenges. Its incredible engineering might was focused on creating great technology, but less focused on a customer problem that needed solving. To make matters worse, the team didn't design cloud services capable of serving a client base whose respective IT estates were all over the place and very different from the environment at Google HQ. When Kurian joined, he quickly set about recruiting customer-facing team members to listen to and communicate the customer requirements to the engineers, as well as to ignite the sales growth they desperately needed. An incredible transformation happened on both fronts, at speed.

In almost no time at all, he took an engineering-led business and placed the customer at the heart of it, showing his team how to engage customers with empathy and how to design products and services to meet their actual needs while operating in the reality of those customers' IT environments. Earlier, I highlighted that you know you're outpacing at this characteristic when your agile technology is delivering a competitive advantage. Clearly, that's what's happening now at GCP.

Pushing hard to disrupt his bigger rivals, Kurian has directed his team to create a welcoming environment for any customer, no matter who they are currently using. He has even gone as far as developing specific services to help clients who want to use multiple cloud providers – a wily move, given that many of GCP's target customers have existing cloud implementations with competitors, while also having considerable more cloud needs in the future. Thomas has enabled GCP to entice clients wanting a choice of cloud providers, but without the handcuffs.

As Google makes up ground on its competitors, Kurian is using its in-house engineering excellence (his tech radar) to set GCP up for the future. At Davos I listened to him impressively articulate how GCP is focused on solving the cloud needs of today's enterprises, before introducing one of his top engineers who talked about the impact quantum computing will have and how Google is already thinking about its application. It became the ultimate visual in my mind. We were right in the center of this radar (with great clarity and control over our current position), but in the distance we could see a small dot labelled "quantum", slowly getting closer to our position. Kurian made it clear that when the time is right, he'll be ready to help GCP customers use it to create a competitive advantage.

As Thomas presses forward, personifying this Outpacer characteristic of being focused on today but preparing for tomorrow, he does so knowing that while he has to drive massive growth, acquiring new customers and market share, he must do so while serving, listening to, learning from and delivering agile technology for his biggest customer and the team that writes his pay check – Google! He may be in third place today, but there's a long way to go. #watchthisspace

WILL.I.AM

He may be best known as a seven-time Grammy-winning musician, but for more than a decade will.i.am has poured his heart, soul and money into the tech sector with an unshakeable belief in the role of technology in all our lives and as a power for good in society.

will.i.am got into tech through his music – literally. The Black Eyed Peas' song "Hey Mama" was used in the first iPod ad campaign in 2003. It was a lightbulb moment for will.i.am: "I was like, 'Wait a second, if they're paying us to sell their stuff, and they're paying us more than it cost to develop it, then I'm going to develop my own stuff and sell it.'" One of his first forays into the world of tech was as a founding shareholder in Beats, which was subsequently bought by Apple for $3.2 billion. His success with Beats would provide him with capital to start what he would go on to refer to as his second career.

I like to break that second career in tech into three parts. Firstly, there is his entrepreneurial work to build tech, both hardware and software, through his own company i.am+. Secondly, there's his evangelizing of the positive potential of tech, particularly around AI, virtual reality, data and robotics. He takes these complex topics and creates a better understanding of the opportunity these technologies can bring to our lives, while also making tech cool. Finally, there's his incredible work to support youth in highly challenging situations to get an education that will help them to get into the tech sector.

will.i.am was raised in the projects, Boyle Heights, in east Los Angeles. It is a predominantly low-income, working-class immigrant community that he describes as rich in culture and potential, but struggling with a lack of resources and opportunities. He is still very connected to his old neighborhood and wants to see opportunities come to those growing up without privilege.

"My mission is to get young people in underserved areas to get excited about technology and learning STEM skills. [. . .] They should aspire to be like the true rockstars of the twenty-first century. [. . .] I tell kids in the hood, 'Don't just try and be like Stevie Wonder, try and be like Steve Jobs.' "

He launched the i.am Angel Foundation in 2009 to transform lives through education, inspiration and opportunity. The foundation helps kids who lack resources to realize their potential. It funds educational programs that focus on STEAM (Science, Technology, Engineering, Arts and Math). It prepares these kids for college and also provides scholarships.

will.i.am's tech radar is absolutely buzzing. He sees incredible innovations in the future through the development of technologies we have today and also yet to be imagined developments that will change our lives. He speaks with passion and perspective on the importance of data, the future of jobs and today's fourth industrial revolution. He is an optimist and a pragmatist, knowing that tech can be a force for good if those most vulnerable in society don't get left behind in acquiring the skills to thrive in this revolution.

He strongly believes that music and tech are entwined together and that the industry that he has topped was founded on technology. "It's the most creative industry in society today," he has said. "Tech is everything. Music is tech. [. . .] If we saw music and tech as the same and not separate, we wouldn't have this gap of [tech] jobs that are unfilled."

Some tech aficionados poke fun at will.i.am for his endeavors in the industry. Personally I welcome someone who brings creativity that I could only dream of, a passion and unrelenting optimism for the power of tech and a rare perspective on how technology can change the lives of everyone in society for the better. Outpacers, with their intellectual curiosity, are keen to explore the views of someone different, whose challenging start in life didn't hold him back from outpacing the music business and taking on the world of tech.

"Look at the world. See the problem. And solve it."

CHAPTER 7

FINANCIAL EXCELLENCE

What does it mean?

Financial management and operations are agile, strategic and aligned to the organization's mVision. The finance team is seen more as a performance coach than a cost-conscious bean-counter. Performance data is easily accessible and enables high performance while also balancing and managing risk. The approach to tax is assured and does not negatively impact the reputation of the company. The organization always understands the value of its assets (in its hands or someone else's) and never stops seeking ways to ensure financial health is maximized. Deal capability is exceptional, allowing swift divestment when appropriate, or acquisition of companies that threaten the business as a competitor or will allow it to accelerate growth beyond the organic plan.

Why is this important?

Clearly you can't run a business with an empty bank account! But to chase an audacious mVision you need a finance team that goes above and beyond keeping the books in order and works seamlessly with the business to provide decision-makers with the kind of "oxygen" they need to make the right decisions. At Outpacer organizations, the finance team uses its position in the organization to enable better decision-making through smart, predictive, data-driven insights. It helps the organization understand the drivers and inhibitors of performance, ultimately assuring delivery of the mVision.

Seriously, this is really important

I get it. You're tempted to skip this chapter because you think it might be a bit dull. Well, you're wrong, and here's why. Think of the finance team as the tires on a racing car. You can have the best engine, an amazing chassis and brilliant aerodynamics, but if your tires aren't excellent, you're not going to win. You may look and sound great (like many aspiring Outpacers), but when you're on the edge needing to maximize performance, the quality of your tires is going to determine whether you are a winner or a loser.

It's the same with your finance team. If you don't see them at that level of criticality, either you've not been lucky enough to work with a team that exudes financial excellence, or you're not making the most of an essential component that is the difference between being first to see the chequered flag and not seeing it at all!

Dynamic duo

Whether your favorite dynamic duo was Batman and Robin, or like me you prefer Michael Jordan and Scottie Pippen, for Outpacers it needs to be your CEO and CFO.

The CEO and CFO need to be joined at the hip and in lock-step, the perfect complement to each other. The CFO needs to be capable of driving change, working alongside a CEO who will welcome it, nurture it and give full support to make it happen. When you get that dynamic right, it's as if you have the accelerator hard to the floor. It's an unstoppable force!

That dynamic duo is so important but it's hard to come by. Quite often there can be friction between the CEO and CFO. It might be that they don't like each other (often the archetypal personalities can clash), or there can be a power struggle, but perhaps the most common reason is that the CFO and their team are not truly valued by the rest of the business. That can be because they're not actually adding value, or because they're not being given the opportunity. Whatever the reason and without being overly dramatic, a negative or dysfunctional relationship between these two leaders will poison the culture of the whole business, permeating into team cohesion and decision-making and causing overall paralysis of the organization. It needs the CEO to recognize that there is a problem that needs fixing, or the Chair or senior non-executive director to step in and make change happen.

One of the most visible impacts of the CEO/CFO dynamic is with investors. According to Bob Cowell, leader of Makinson Cowell, who have been surveying the world's biggest investors for decades, "investors know that one of the key determinants of a positive upward share price trajectory in any business is the relationship between the CEO and CFO. A great dynamic will result in stability, speedy and unified decision-making, better ability to cope with a crisis, a higher likelihood of achieving the company's goals and therefore achieving a great return for shareholders."

Investor relations

Most Outpacers have a respectful but healthy suspicion that the capital markets will try to drive to a short-term agenda. As I mentioned in the first chapter, Outpacers are not deaf to comments made, but won't be deviated from their course, especially for the sake of short-term gains. But clearly investors cannot be ignored, and it's down to finance to tread the line between confidence and arrogance.

One simple solution is to get the *right* investors on board from the outset. Outpacers are organizations that have a passion and belief in what they do, and have every intention of continuing to do it – whatever it is – for the long term. They need investors with a similar outlook. Whether you're a public or private company, shareholders that are desperate for an outcome will create pressure that will be very uncomfortable for you if you're not aligned.

Are you doing appropriate due diligence on the way that a potential investor wants to work? Are these potential investors aligned to your strategy and trajectory? Are they looking for a quick exit strategy with a significant return on investment? They will be doing due diligence on you – don't forget to perform reverse due diligence on them.

It can be tempting and flattering to have people willing to invest in you. If your idea is that good and you're set to become an Outpacer, you should have a queue of investors and you shouldn't be beholden to any particular one. It might sound harsh, but if you've only got one main investor interested, then maybe your idea isn't as good as you think.

What finance does

The roles performed by finance should in my view be strategic. Within this team you have some of the finest and brightest commercial finance talent and they should be fully focused on the biggest and hairiest challenges for the business.

While in many traditional corporates the finance team can be landed with other responsibilities like IT, facilities or payroll, I don't think they necessarily should be. This is no slight on these functions, which play a pivotal role in the business, but they don't require a CFO to manage them and you want your finance team focused on what only they can do – they're there to maximize performance.

If the CFO is spending time on sorting out the internal IT network, that individual is not really being optimized. In my view the CFO would be better off saying no to anything that's not core and remaining focused on the critical role they play. If you want to outpace, every individual needs to be doing what only they can do. The caveat to this is when the CFO is being lined up as the CEO's successor, so the CEO and Board want to give the CFO the opportunity to lead non-finance areas of the business to see how it goes. The point still remains that if that's what's happening, then the CFO is distracted and needs to ensure their successor is fully focused on the core finance job at hand, which in my view should cover the following:

- Accounting
- Financial Planning & Analysis (FP&A)
- Strategy, and Mergers & Acquisitions (M&A)
- Performance (often called "controllership")
- Investor Relations
- Tax
- Procurement (Sourcing)
- Risk/Governance (but more of that in Chapter 8)

It's the way finance delivers on these key areas that marks out the difference between outpacing and being an also-ran. For many companies the day-to-day accounting is a lot. Combine that with being profitable and compliant with all the various global accounting regulations, and it already takes a huge effort. Any misstep in accounting regulations, even if at an early stage of corporate life, will come back to haunt you. Potential investors won't trust an organization with significant investment if it's not capable of sorting the business as usual. But in Outpacers, finance teams take this in their stride and are looking beyond today, into their long-term plan. They understand the mVision and the actions required of them to help reach the destination, not just the year end. They have started to apply traditional accounting and controllership skills to data science, process excellence and relationship and business performance management, leading to long-term value creation.

Let's spend some time talking about the ways in which finance must deliver for you to be an Outpacer organization, and how you can help.

Oxygen

Without oxygen we can't survive. And the richer, clearer and less contaminated the oxygen supply, the better it is for us. In an Outpacer, it's finance that provides that rich oxygen to every aspect of the organization, allowing it not just to breathe, but to breathe deeply. Higher-quality oxygen going into the organization drives performance.

With countless critical decisions to be made, it can be hard to actually stop, take those deep breaths and give yourself time to assess the situation before continuing forward. In an Outpacer, financial excellence is epitomized by that pure oxygen boost in the form of the unique data insights presented to the business that no one else spotted (or had the time to spot). That boost is the analysis of leading indicators that then enable the business to find an edge in the marketplace.

In an Outpacer the finance team has a seat at the table for every important business interaction and decision right from the start, to bring the insights that are most pertinent to the business. It's in everyone's interest that finance is involved in critical decision-making. Every individual at the table needs the oxygen that the finance team provides, to ensure the conversation is rich and full of data-driven insights that are aligned to the mVision.

They also need to be equipped with the best tools for the job. For all good reasons, Outpacers put product first, which often means prioritizing internal resources – including data analytics capability and software investment – for front-office teams. For an engineering powerhouse, the default will often be to think that finance can be serviced by a home-grown software solution. But rather than make finance wait in line, Outpacers are prepared to look at all options, including buying something that they could build themselves, in order for finance to have the right tools, in the right timeframe.

None of this will happen if finance itself doesn't step up and see its role as a change agent, rather than a steady pair of hands. Finance cannot be subservient to the business. It must show the value that it can add and by doing so secure buy-in from the business units and a permanent seat at the table. As a change agent, it may implement steps that will be disruptive and create short-term pain for business units used to "the way we do things". It's the job of finance to spot how a course correction might be required for the business to stay on track and to have the assertiveness to call those changes, and it must have executive support for implementation regardless of the disruption. In many ways, it needs to coach the business, communicating the value of making change and improving overall performance. Which brings me to the next role . . .

Performance coach

Most finance teams have "controllers". While I fully understand the history and intention of the title, my experience is that in Outpacer organizations they are less of a controller and more of an enabler. At their best they're enabling maximum business performance. They are a performance coach.

Stereotyping is a dangerous activity, and while this is not always the case, often the somewhat more reserved finance team member can be intimidated by the flamboyant and charismatic product manager or sales leader who's far more interested in telling than listening. It's in these situations that the performance coach comes to the fore, encouraging that individual to stop talking, receive vital information and have the chance to fulfil their potential.

I guarantee that those who do stop and listen to the coach will feel the benefits. Decisions on where investments will be made to reach the mVision rely on multi-function input with product management, strategy and finance working together. If a product manager is looking for additional investment, finance should be working with them to help prove (or disprove) the return on that investment for shareholders. This slight shift in focus towards shareholders is key in getting teams to think beyond their immediate needs and more about overall performance and outcomes. Insightful questions can help product and front-office teams understand the key metrics the business is held to account on, and what they need to achieve in order to secure their investment.

Not everyone in the business is a financial whizz, but every action and decision has an impact on the financial success of the business. Ask the right questions and the team can raise the financial IQ of the organization, making everyone appreciate the standards that are expected for successful investment and the role that finance has to play. Business units that listen to the coach, change their behavior and do what is required are more likely to be rewarded when investment decisions are made.

The very best coaches are also up to speed on the latest techniques to unlock potential. For financial excellence, that includes using technology to optimize performance.

A good example of this would be the use of automation. As the coach, the finance team is looking at the end-to-end impact that automation can deliver for the business. They see that it's more than just a cost-saving exercise for a certain process. It's change and transformation to help the whole team run faster.

The non-Outpacer takes a process – let's use FP&A as an example – that has relatively high headcount of, let's say, 100 people. The finance team excitedly throws automation technology at the process to reduce headcount. In a matter of months, fifty heads at $75,000 per annum are no longer required, and with lower operation cost and very low business disruption as a result of keeping the process the same as before, this feels like a project well done.

The Outpacer looks at the same FP&A function and, in collaboration with the key business stakeholders, re-engineers the process and target operating model end to end, optimizing for internal and external users before applying the automation technology that ultimately creates the same headcount reduction opportunity.

But it doesn't stop there. The Outpacer now decides on one of two options. The employees who are no longer required for the automated process can be redeployed to roles that can better use their skills – they are still devoted talent who have signed up to the mVision, after all. Instead of banking the savings from the headcount reduction, twenty data scientists are hired at $150,000 per annum, who take the data from the new FP&A process and transform the insights delivered to the business, enabling faster and better decision-making. The result? The non-Outpacer saved money in the short term, but lost out massively in the long term, cheating the overall business out of what it actually needed.

The scary thing is that too many executives accept the non-Outpacer example. Worse still, they even reward the delivery. This short-sighted outlook happens every day in businesses around the world. But it doesn't happen at an Outpacer because the finance team is performance-coaching every day to ensure sustainable greatness rather than a short-term, one-off success. Finance is the change agent in the business and the ultimate enabler of the change required in every market, every product and every geography.

It's that flywheel again. Once finance is enabling high performance, the rest of the business wants them at the table as much as they want to be there. Success breeds success, with finance delivering breakthrough coaching to colleagues that ensures everyone is outpacing.

Private equity lens

I have a deep admiration for the PE (private equity) industry. I'm probably not in the majority. Many see PE companies as pariahs for their perceived harsh action, often taking out large amounts of cost as they transform the businesses they own.

In my view, they are like special forces in the military: expert, elite teams that quickly and decisively take necessary actions to achieve an outcome that is extremely challenging or nigh on impossible. Special forces don't see insurmountable obstacles. After all, "who dares wins"! They pursue goals and outcomes where the reward is high, but the risk is great.

Obviously no one in private equity is putting their life on the line, but they are putting considerable capital to work in a high-risk, high-reward scenario. It's not just fearless pursuit of these challenges that I admire, it's the methodical and disciplined way in which the outcome is achieved. You need the same traits to be an Outpacer.

In an Outpacer, the finance function wears more than one hat. There's the necessity to keep an eye on the core business and make sure that the everyday is being achieved. Every business, Outpacer or not, needs stability and control from finance. But there's also the need to simultaneously take a far more strategic role and see that the right investments are being made for the future. This is the private equity lens, where finance needs to understand and recognize relevant market trends and disruptors, and be prepared to add investments (some with a degree of risk) to the portfolio to enable innovation that will transform the business.

I mentioned the FP&A function earlier. In many businesses, innovation efforts are funded through an annual budgeting process. Innovation is not something that can be scheduled to sit neatly within an annual cycle. Competitors posing a threat or strategic acquisitions won't wait for the next budget round. Instead, think like private equity and be ready to move when an opportunity presents itself. Outpacing finance teams find it much easier to make quick decisions as and when required, not as and when it suits internal processes.

Knowing which investments are the right investments is another key trait for an outpacing finance team. Working with the business units, and with a clear eye on potential changes in the marketplace, they'll be able to manage the portfolio in such a way that riskier investments are balanced with ongoing investments that support the core business. Pulling off that particular balancing act requires a different mindset. Traditional finance teams might look at an investment in terms of revenue or ROI (return on investment), potentially sealing its fate before it has had a chance to shine. Outpacers look at those metrics in the context of the mVision, using data-driven insights to make bold moves with confidence, secure in their knowledge of the scenarios and outcomes most likely to happen.

Investment decisions are not shots in the dark but, as with special forces operations, coolly calculated, without emotion. Too often, organizations are democratic in their funding and the tough decisions don't get taken. Emotional attachments are formed to businesses they have been involved with for a number of years. A CEO can feel paternal towards a business they have spent years developing and nurturing, dishing out investment more equally than they should, no matter what the analysis says. The trait of an Outpacer, and the private equity industry, is to take out the emotion and simply ask where they are getting the best return. That disciplined, rigorous approach sets them apart from the pack.

Mergers and acquisitions strategy

Whether it's to build and extend capability faster than is possible through organic growth, increase geographic coverage or achieve greater scale, M&A is a common growth strategy. Yet according to the *Harvard Business Review*, 70–90 per cent of mergers and acquisitions fail. It's an understatement to say that this area is performing poorly but it's something that Outpacers do well. Cisco has completed over 200 acquisitions and reports that over 80 per cent of acquired employees are still with the company three years later.

There are many elements to a successful acquisition, but realizing synergy gains is right up there. In an Outpacer, the finance team is critical in ensuring that what is purchased will fit with operations and that the synergies hoped for will be achieved. However, it would be a very tall order for them to ensure that the integration will meet those synergies if they weren't consulted at the beginning and could not advise on complementary strengths and weaknesses. Think of an M&A like a player transfer. If the coach doesn't know how best to use the new player or they are not integrated properly into the team because their strengths and weaknesses are not fully understood, it might change the dynamic for the worse.

It's worth bearing in mind that a successful M&A strategy can be as much about divestment as it is about acquisition. After years of digging deep into its capacious pockets, Google's parent company Alphabet raised $5.7 billion in external funding for its autonomous driving business, Waymo. Alphabet took the decision to divest in part and share the ownership with venture capitalists who are invested for long-term returns. As a result, they benefit from the additional expertise provided by the new investors and have reduced the amount of capital they had tied up (while still retaining control), capital that can be redeployed to other investment opportunities elsewhere. Importantly, it keeps investors who can see the benefit of a mixed short- and long-term strategy onside.

MAKING THE INVESTMENT CASE

A word about M&A strategy and buying up competitors. There is no doubt that acquiring dangerous competitors before they become dangerous is a potential strategy – as I mentioned in Chapter 4 on Collaborative Innovation, it's about survival of the fittest, eat or be eaten. There's equally no doubt that because of the risk of stifling competition, it's controversial and several companies are already in the crosshairs of the competition authorities. But it would be wrong to paint a picture of small innovative companies constantly being crushed by villainous Outpacers with swooshing dark cloaks. Google's $2.1 billion acquisition of Fitbit is a good example of a different narrative. On its own, Fitbit had gone as far as it could go and was losing ground to much larger competitors such as Apple, possibly heading towards extinction. The acquisition will allow the two companies to work together to produce better products to support health and wellness needs. It creates a competitive check with Apple, so ticks increasing competition as well.

DYNAMIC SAT NAV/GPS

When I moved to California I started using Waze (other sat navs/GPSs are also available!). The roads were all new to me, many of the journeys I was taking were time pressured (you can't be late for your sons' football matches) and the traffic was dreadful. I really like Waze because it gets me to where I need to go as quickly and safely as possible. I don't need to listen out for traffic reports and try to figure out other route options because it will reroute me automatically. It even alerts me to dangers on my road, keeping me, my passengers and other road users safe. It optimizes my journey in real time, I completely trust the analysis and recommendations and ultimately it delivers a service for me that makes me more efficient and effective.

To achieve financial excellence, the finance team needs to act like a dynamic sat nav/GPS for the entire business. The mVision has been set, the destination is clear, but there is no chance the route that is initially set as the way to get there will remain the same. There are simply too many things that will change along the way, both obstacles and opportunities. A bit like my Waze, the finance team is there to ensure that every opportunity is taken to optimize the journey and that the destination is reached in the best manner possible. What that means in practice is that data on the journey (i.e. performance) needs to be accessible and visible all the time and dynamic decision recommendations for the next best action must be presented by finance in real time, based on the constantly changing environment.

The things that can throw you off kilter can come in all shapes and sizes and from any direction. It could be competitors launching new products, new regulatory impacts, geopolitical events such as a change in government or new laws and regulations. It can be as extreme as a global pandemic, or sometimes as simple as focusing so hard in one direction that you fail to see what's coming up in the rearview mirror.

Take Facebook's move to mobile. For years, the company's focus was on its desktop service, and all new developments were built with a laptop or PC in mind. What they failed to spot until it was almost too late was that the target audience was switching to smartphones and mobile devices. Facebook's mVision is to bring the world closer together through secure communication. If its audience was on mobile, then it would need to switch too. Keeping on their course of desktop focus, and not deviating, would most likely have allowed competitors with a presence on mobile to steal their audience and ultimately suffocated the business. While it may seem obvious with hindsight, redirecting the entire company to focus on mobile was a very significant strategic move. Think of a bricks and mortar retailer diverting its entire focus to online and digital. It felt risky at the time – particularly for a soon-to-be-public tech company. As Sheryl Sandberg, COO of Facebook, reports, "We had no mobile revenue, not a little bit, none, and I'm looking at Mark [Zuckerberg] and saying, 'No one can fire you and only you can fire me, so if you're in, I'm in.'" As part of the shift Zuckerberg solely used his mobile and encouraged his teams to do the same, and the company hired new iOS and Android engineers, held extensive bootcamps to get their existing employees up to speed and embedded mobile engineers into every product team at the company.

In this example, I'm not suggesting that finance made the call. What I am saying is that this is a great example of the kind of opportunity finance can spot (using the data-driven insights) and highlight to help change the business trajectory. It's also the case that this kind of transformation would have been inconceivable without a finance team being 100 per cent on board and having the ability to make a fast shift, moving all their investment and resources to focus on a new direction.

There are many events that can have dramatic and profound impacts on the outlook of a business. Sometimes the right thing to do is to stay cool and not overreact, while sometimes you need to move fast and react decisively. The key thing is making the right decision and that's down to your ability to trust and get input and advice from your finance team.

When your sat nav recommends an alternative route to you, it effectively takes reams of data and comes up with a better option that you may or may not accept. Ultimately your sat nav is not in charge. You are. That is the same in business. If you're running a business and your finance team suggests a different route from the one you were planning, you know that team has the data and insights that often allow you to make better decisions. They are your partner at the table, so you listen.

Reaching Outpacer status is a pretty monumental achievement. It doesn't happen overnight and sustaining it is really tough. Although there is a destination, in reality you're on a constant, never-ending journey and you need your dynamic sat nav for every step of this epic trip. I wouldn't dream of driving without my sat nav, and you shouldn't dream of running your business or taking decisions without your finance team by your side.

Thrifty

In an Outpacer, the CFO and their team are thrifty as opposed to frugal. A thrifty person doesn't waste much water, energy or money. In contrast, a frugal person uses as little of everything as possible. One of Amazon's leadership principles is frugality, so they may not agree with me, but as I see it, for most it's not about spending as little as possible, but about spending the right amount and not wasting precious dollars.

For many Outpacers, the benefit of their success is having stacks of cash! So why the need to be thrifty? The answer is that if you start spending like you're a baller, you'll lose the DNA that got you where you are in the first place and you'll fall off a cliff.

There's a great example enshrined in Amazon folklore. In the early days, Jeff Bezos took an old door and fixed wooden 4x4 legs with a couple of brackets to hold it all together to create his own "door desk". Of course this was a good way to save a few dollars when starting a business on a shoestring budget but they continued to use them (and continue to this day in some offices). They were totemic of one of Amazon's core principles: money should be spent on making things better for their customers. The door desk also exemplifies a way of cutting costs that almost no other company would think of, and finding those ideas that help Amazon bring down their costs is at the heart of their day-to-day mission. Of course Amazon spend money on research and development to get an edge, but the door desk is an example of one of their leadership principles: "Constraints breed resourcefulness, self-sufficiency, and invention." The door desk is Amazon accomplishing more with less.

Netflix's expense policy is another example. The policy is simple: "Act in Netflix's best interest." Netflix places extensive trust in their employees' judgment – in their eyes, if they're the right person for the job, they should have the judgment that goes along with the importance of that role. Therefore, Netflix gives their employees pretty much full autonomy over expenses (although of course, all expenses could be reviewed at any time) and the rule is simple: if an expense would benefit Netflix, then do it. If it would be a profligate use of company money without justification, then don't. The policy is a winner on two counts. In line with its culture and vision, Netflix encourages responsibility, while recognizing that people are inclined to spend less when the responsibility lies in their hands. Secondly, it dispenses with the need for countless time-wasting approvals from someone's senior.

In both examples above, taking a thrifty approach encourages behaviors that are in line with each company's mVision. Attempting to be frugal can have the polar opposite effect and actually cause reputational damage. Paying tax is a prime example. There are opportunities for many organizations to take a short-term decision that reduces the amount of tax being paid. But taking that approach isn't sustainable. Tax goes way beyond a spreadsheet and has an impact on your brand, and on your reputation in the community you serve.

Big tech has been heavily criticized for its approach to tax, but in the face of widespread condemnation, we are seeing a change of tack. The agreement to set a global minimum corporate tax rate of at least 15 per cent was welcomed by Google and Facebook, who highlighted the benefits to all of a transparent and consistent system. Tax breaks offered during the global pandemic, for example to furlough canteen staff, were declined. Big tech has matured and has a renewed sense of their responsibility to give back.

Tax is an extremely technical area and can often be siloed off to a separate team. It's important for finance leadership to ensure that tax doesn't become isolated. When finance has clear sight and responsibility over options being pursued, the temptation to veer from the mVision for short-term benefit is less likely to arise.

Procurement is another area where companies can be tempted to fall into frugality. Outpacers don't squeeze suppliers to the point where they might start cutting corners to keep their costs down. The credentials that come from working with a big brand mean that suppliers would be prepared to do so. But, as Uncle Ben in *Spider-Man* (and a great many illustrious people before him) once said, "with great power comes great responsibility".

Outpacers have a responsibility to make sure they are creating a sustainable ecosystem that does not exploit suppliers. That doesn't mean at the expense of good prices. A good price can still be a win–win for both parties. Outpacers are able to create a healthy ecosystem where all ships are rising in the port.

At Outpacer organizations, finance is behind the decisions that drive top-line growth and margin improvement, as well as cost management. It sits at the top table, providing the oxygen required for the senior leadership team to be able to make business-critical decisions. It acts as the enabler to maximize business potential and is up to speed on the latest technology to optimize performance. It acts as a change agent, performance coach and private equity advisor, all the while ensuring that in the race to outpace, the CFO and CEO are running side by side and not being forced into a short-term agenda by investors. It's pretty clear to see that, when given the right resources and authority, finance is critical to your success as an Outpacer.

RUTH PORAT

Named as "Best Financial Institutions CFO", also as one of the most powerful women in business by both *Forbes* and *Fortune* magazines, and rumored to be one of President Obama's picks for Treasury Secretary, look no further than Ruth Porat for our Outpacer for financial excellence.

She has been the Chief Financial Officer of Alphabet Inc. and its subsidiary Google since 2015, following a long and successful career in investment banking, where she ultimately became CFO of Morgan Stanley.

If you listen to Ruth and to Google CEO Sundar Pichai, they are in lock-step, a dynamic duo committed to the mVision. One of the best examples was the full support she received for unpopular changes. She even acquired the nickname "Ruth-less" for her financial rigor, famously including the cost of employee stock options in managers' budgets. Having achieved the kind of financial results most companies dream of, her nickname has changed to "Ruth-full". Google needed a CFO of Ruth's caliber, and she joined a mission she was excited about, in a business she knew well, having invested in an angel fund in 1998 and worked on the initial public offering in 2004. That close proximity, knowledge and experience increased the chances of forming a dynamic duo and was no doubt a big contributor to the chemistry witnessed in the boardroom and overall the Outpacing success at Alphabet.

Ruth is a big proponent of investing in the future, stating, "If you don't invest in the long term, you are literally sowing the seeds of your own destruction." Having been at the top of her game on Wall Street for thirty years, her views carry significant gravitas. I believe investors are now more open than ever to a longer-term value creation play and that Ruth has played a key role in this greater understanding.

But it's not a blank check from investors to Ruth, nor is it a blank check from Ruth to her fellow Googlers. She has taken a less rebellious approach to managing Wall Street than some other public big tech companies. Perhaps those years on the other side provide her with more sympathy for the analysts who have to build the financial models to create their forecasts! They have Ruth to thank for an increase in financial reporting transparency that is shown to Alphabet investors, such as breaking out the earnings in businesses such as Cloud and YouTube.

One of the biggest challenges for the CFO of an Outpacer is to stay financially disciplined and hungry. Porat will tell you that you must "anchor everything in data, and the rest will follow", so decisions don't come from a hunch, but are born out of data-driven insights that are transparent and clear for all to see. This approach leads to greater consensus and is likely to drive investing in the best areas. When it comes to ensuring that no one gets carried away with the huge amount of cash on hand, she describes using the budgetary process to ensure "there is a tight enough resource envelope to drive discussions [with those running those businesses] on how to self-fund businesses. [. . .] They know what they want to prioritize. Get the discussion with the business partners with the greatest insights on where to place bets and where they think the greatest opportunity is."

Two things strike me. The first is the idea that no matter how much cash there is, you create a "tight enough resource envelope" to force disciplined prioritization. The second is the empowerment to drive decision-making by those with the most expertise to make a call on it, those closest to the customer. It is without doubt the recipe for success.

Porat's financial rigor has allowed Alphabet to successfully scale beyond the expectations of almost everyone. Finance plays a clear and pivotal role in enabling brilliant decision-making by brilliant people, driven by transparent data that allows for prioritization and ensures, in the words of former Google CEO Larry Page, that there is "more wood behind fewer arrows". Porat has enabled that brilliantly.

OPRAH

One of the key tenets of this book, and of being an Outpacer, is achieving astonishingly high levels of performance across all nine characteristics. Oprah Winfrey could be our Outpacer icon for almost any of our characteristics, but I've chosen financial excellence. It may seem surprising, but I've done so because one of her many lessons to us is that if you focus just on the financial outcome, you won't be rich in any sense of the word.

Oprah says, "The reason I've been able to be so financially successful is my focus has never, not for one minute, been money." It's a great reminder that to achieve financial excellence you must have total flow with all Outpacer elements, and a clear purpose – why everyone turns up for work each day. Oprah is recognized for her impact on people and her caring and empathetic nature, rather than being defined by her wealth. Every day she delivers on her mVision, and her pursuit of a great purpose – coupled with her incredible business acumen – has led her to amass a fortune. (Oprah was the first Black woman to host a TV show, at age 19, and to later go on to become a billionaire.)

There are very few people who can talk with such courage and conviction on their purpose as Oprah. She describes a moment of clarity while interviewing members of the KKK (who she was trying to expose on national TV), when she realized that she was the one being used. It drove her to start "using TV as a platform to speak to the world". She asked her team, "How do we want to see the world change? How do we want to impact the world? Let all shows be focused and centered around that." From then on, content decisions were made on the intention behind the programming, and this intention-fueled and purposeful programming was key to their success.

Bringing that back to financial excellence, the lesson I take away is that you can do all the right things to run the perfect finance team, but if that's done in a vacuum of purpose, it's not going to work.

Another key trait of Oprah's is her investment in herself and her audience. She invests in and connects with her audience on a deep and personal level, while also having fun. She has spread unrelenting joy with expensive gifts to loyal fans and deserving individuals, from free cars to shelter and new homes for those left devastated by Hurricane Katrina. She is also clear on the importance of investing in yourself first. In a play on words, she talks about the importance of being "full of yourself". Oprah's view is that only once your cup is full to overflowing can you really give the best of yourself. She says, do not be afraid to "honor yourself" as that is "your reason for being here." Take note. That means investing in yourself and allowing your people to do the same, so that everyone is "full of themselves"!

Oprah's glasses also have a superb PE lens on them. Her incredible talent and entrepreneurial flair for building, optimizing and identifying business growth are unquestionable. Oprah was at the height of her TV career success when she left her legendary talk show to launch her own channel, The Oprah Winfrey Network (OWN). She also invested in other ventures, including: being one of the first into the Oxygen network, a women-orientated channel; founding *O, The Oprah Magazine*; starting the Oprah's Book Club segment; investing in Weight Watchers, which surged in value with her involvement; and being a founding producer for Apple TV+ (and this list doesn't come close to covering it all). This incredible woman loves challenges, is happy to take on risk, is not afraid of failure and invests in businesses that she understands and that are aligned to a purposeful intention. Through these traits, which are critical to financial excellence, she has amassed a fortune. In her words, "I had no idea that being your authentic self could make me as rich as I've become. If I had, I'd have done it a lot earlier."

CHAPTER 8

ENABLING GOVERNANCE

What does that really mean?

Enabling governance allows the business to be truly excellent in all areas, keeping employees safe, ensuring the company is compliant with all legal and regulatory requirements and maintaining a highly trusted reputation with all stakeholders. The company understands the connected nature of risks and monitors them in a dynamic fashion. The governance framework does not create bureaucracy, but rather instills a high level of accountability that enables the entrepreneurial culture by ensuring risks are understood and decisions taken in an informed and calculated manner. Financial controls are tightly maintained and audits are transparent, with standards and practices above industry expectations.

Why is this important?

Enabling governance allows the business to focus on its strategic imperatives by minimizing distraction caused by unforeseen operational issues. In today's rapidly changing competitive environment, businesses do not have time to pause while they sort out a digression or failure. Risks must be properly managed to minimize the potential for disruption to either operations or reputations. Outpacers recognize that smart, appropriate and practical governance is key to enabling success. Everyone in an Outpacer organization – from senior leadership and cascaded throughout the business – believes that governance is as much about achieving the highest quality as it is about a bunch of rules that must be obeyed.

Just the word governance is often enough to have wannabe Outpacers wanting to change the subject to something they see as more important – like growth. I understand that. The word can conjure up catastrophic failures such as Enron, WorldCom or Lehman Brothers – and the resulting legislation (Sarbanes–Oxley being one example, following in the wake of Enron) with which well-meaning organizations are subsequently obliged to comply. There are many businesses that think compliance is just a box-ticking exercise to appease external audiences, feeling safe in the knowledge that they have no intention of acting fraudulently or negligently. Even worse, they believe it's someone else's job and the rest of the business reluctantly has to go along with it, then move on. The point that's being missed is that the right approach to governance will not only prevent you from becoming a statistic, but also allow you to set a tone of excellence in the business, building trust with stakeholders and maximizing – yes, maximizing – the risks that can be taken to support entrepreneurial culture and delivery of the mVision.

Enabling governance is more about your culture, your values and what's in your DNA. To outpace, ask yourself what kind of business you are today, and what you want to be when you grow up. Sure, you need the right programs and processes, but they won't succeed in isolation. You have to commit time, energy and focus to make it work. It's a bit like committing to getting into shape. If your diet and exercise regime are consistently good because they matter to you, you'll succeed. But if you neglect them, or just pay lip service to them with the odd two-mile run (quarterly review), you'll never get there.

Marching to your own drum

Taking comfort from the fact that their business practices and ethical stance are above board, many think that being compliant is good enough. Some have the view that the point of compliance is to comply with the rules, and as long as that is happening, all is well. In an Outpacer, that's not the case. That laissez-faire attitude sails contrary to their beliefs, as by merely obeying a set of rules, they are not setting the standards. And that's what Outpacers do.

Earlier I talked about creating the mVision and I looked at the importance of values and creating a purposeful organization. There is a pressure and demand from top talent for the organizations in which they work to have a moral compass on key topics and for their work to actually do something for the greater good. It's really not a leap to say that the governance, compliance and risk framework are linked to those values and that sense of purpose. Standards need to be, where relevant, above the regulations. Outpacers drive the highest level of quality in the organization and align to something purposeful that is doing great things in the broader economy and society.

To be an Outpacer, it's not as simple as picking and choosing the things you want to excel at. Your greatness needs to permeate throughout your organization in everything you do.

Better quality performance

Just as Outpacers want a sense of purpose to run through an organization, so too the highest level of quality needs to touch every area. If everything is running to the highest standard possible, the quality of the business will be higher.

In an environment in which governance is an enabler rather than a handicap, the role of internal audit and other risk and compliance teams is more than just ensuring that everyone's in line. It's also about pushing the boundaries of quality and continuous improvement.

Imagine this scenario: your organization is undergoing a large tech implementation that will have ramifications across existing systems and the internal audit team is sent in to conduct a review. In a non-Outpacer, that team will probably be given the run-around. They are most likely viewed as the internal police and treated with, at best, tolerance. The value derived by the team on the receiving end of their advice is often questioned. The biggest priority is to get them out and onto the next thing as fast as possible, preferably with a glowing report saying "no problem here".

If you're an Outpacer, you'll welcome the team, recognizing that they have expertise that will benefit the business. You will embrace the individuals who are experts in this particular technology implementation and can give advice on how the plan could go one step higher if their recommendations were taken on. Without their advice, you would probably be fine, but how can you be better? The team on the receiving end brings an intellectual curiosity to the process. They don't see it as criticism, but ask what they can learn from this team and how they can maximize their chances of success. It's about being collaborative, not combative. All in all a higher-quality outcome is achieved than would have been possible without the intervention.

In the financial excellence section, we talked about performance coaching and the role of the finance team in encouraging individuals to listen, take advice and improve performance. That's exactly the way risk and compliance teams should be operating and perceived by the business.

Avoid disasters

One way to avoid disasters is to invest ahead of the curve, or learn quickly from an incident and invest to ensure there's no repeat. Having governance systems in place that are appropriate to your business activities can flag up trouble before it strikes. When your growth is exponential, it can be hard and expensive to cover every base, but that doesn't mean you'll get any let-up if something goes wrong. Facebook was famously fined $5 billion to settle privacy concerns following allegations that Cambridge Analytica, a political consultancy, improperly obtained data on up to 87 million Facebook users. There was recognition that the cost to the company did not stop there. Facebook's head of global affairs, Sir Nick Clegg, stated that when it came to regaining the public's trust, "I don't think people are going to take the assurances from Facebook that all will be well in the future – I don't think words are enough." Facebook went on to overhaul its approach to privacy. Influential board director Roxanne Austin calls this "ROR" – return of reputation. As she says, "The risk of (and cost to repair) damage to the reputation of the enterprise trump the traditional ROI discussions we use to justify projects or investments. The time and money spent to repair the damage after a major incident (ROR) is staggering." When you factor in the cost of dealing with the legal, regulatory, customer, employee and financial impact of a reputational disaster, it becomes clear that investing in an appropriate governance framework isn't optional and will help avoid disasters happening in the first place.

Build trust

If you fail to be compliant in something as relatively straightforward as the way you conduct your financial affairs, the trust that your stakeholders and investors have in your business will be undermined. Trust is a quality that's hard to gain and easy to lose. Organizations are judged on their performance across many areas, and customers will not trust your products if you are seen to be breaching privacy rules, for example. Taking the opposite approach, however, is not only sustainable, but advantageous.

Apple increasingly uses privacy and trust as a key differentiator from its competitors. It even likes to take a dig every now and then. Its slogan "What happens on your iPhone stays on your iPhone" (a take on the classic line "What happens in Vegas stays in Vegas"), posted on a huge billboard in Las Vegas where the Consumer Electronics Show was being held, is a great example. The company has successfully made the link between privacy and trust with its broader stakeholders, positioning itself as an organization that operates to the highest quality. This has been so successful that Apple is now moving beyond using its stance on privacy as a marketing message on corporate values. Privacy-related features now appear as a core part of new products and support expansion into new markets such as online payments, identity and health. Apple wants users to feel more comfortable using its products, knowing that when it comes to this more sensitive information, they can trust Apple and its approach. Consumers who trust an organization and believe it operates to the highest standard are more likely to reward it with their hard-earned cash.

Better risk-taking

Outpacers know that they have to take risks to move forward. Their approach is to ensure that they are known and calculated risks that won't compromise the organization. It's not that they necessarily want to be exposed to risk, but they know that without pushing the boundaries of what's possible, the business won't be able to innovate and push ahead. In an enabling governance environment, the role of the risk and compliance teams is to help safely push those boundaries, rather than pull them in tighter, striving for quality and continuous improvement.

If you're thinking about taking risk (and you have to), having the right governance framework and using the right tools will give you a much better idea of how much risk you're actually taking, and therefore improve your risk decision-making. Predictive modelling and use of data will allow you to see what's likely to happen if you press ahead. Today's entrepreneurs, often backed by venture capital, are far more reliant on data in terms of their decision-making. The reality is that behind the scenes, risk is being constantly reduced through better insights, better data and better predictive models that allow these organizations to predict a number of different scenarios that might occur and be prepared for any one of them. As a result, they are not caught off guard. There's no stepping into the dark, relying on gut instinct or a wing and a prayer. Because of the levels of transparency and clarity, the pros and cons of taking that risk are clear to see.

Let's take another scenario: a business is considering investing in a new region, for example the Middle East, led by the product team, who see a large market opportunity, with huge demand and significant growth potential. The board are more reticent, citing a difficult and unfamiliar environment. There is the potential for a lot of procrastination, with people sitting on the fence and a decision being delayed. Within an enabling governance framework, governance uses technology and data analytics to make a quick evaluation of any risks and also provide potential mitigations for each. They make a swift decision supporting the product team, providing them with a framework within which to operate, covering, for example, the business's position on diversity, which came out as a top risk when they ran the analysis. There is total clarity for the team on the ground, and the board are confident that the risks have been assessed and will be constantly reviewed. The governance framework has enabled the business to make a quick and positive move forward.

The right governance and risk framework around your business should allow you to maximize the risk you take with the highest amount of clarity on the scenarios likely to come your way, and enable your entrepreneurial culture to thrive. Remember that I pointed out in Chapter 2 that combining entrepreneurial culture with sound processes and deep experience is crucial for Outpacers. Governance and culture are inextricably linked. An outpacing culture will allow you to set the framework that represents and reflects your values and standards without compromising your entrepreneurial character. If you already have a suffocating, risk-averse governance framework, it will already be stifling creativity and innovation and have created a culture of "no". The bad news is that a "no" culture will smother the best strategy every day. Even if the CEO and board say they want to be entrepreneurial and become an Outpacer, it will be impossible while their governance model is archaic and suffocating.

When to do it

It's tempting to say, "My biggest priority is to get my valuation up and I'll worry about sorting out governance later." At the non-Outpacer, often the governance model has been in place for years, without anything going wrong. In the frenzied world we live in, the phrase "if it ain't broke, don't fix it" rings true and there always seem to be more important things to focus on. And to a degree that's understandable. But hoping that what is in place will see you through or that you won't be tested is hardly a sustainable plan. You can't wait for things to go badly wrong. Bear in mind that when they do, it's normally the CEO or other senior members of the executive team that depart.

The level of scrutiny on the tech sector is increasing every day. Given its dominant role in the economy and society, it's easy to forget that this is a relatively young and immature sector and set of organizations. With this greater role has come greater responsibility and, hand in hand with that, much greater scrutiny.

I know firsthand that these Outpacers recognize that potentially their biggest derailer is a breach of their own governance standards, rules and regulations. They know that they're in the spotlight and that their reputation relies on them getting this right. To the press, regulators and many more besides, they are a target, and therefore the way they operate has to be to the highest standard all the time.

If you're an Outpacer today, the level of scrutiny tomorrow will be significantly higher. The starting gun to get the governance framework in place has definitely already gone off. You need to work through the people, process and cultural changes required and ensure alignment with the mVision. Get it right in the early stages and reap the benefits, rather than being forced to implement a framework as a result of a crisis caused by a failure in risk and governance.

Focus and prioritization

You might ask why I didn't include this whole section in Chapter 7 on Financial Excellence (although you'll note that I did capture it as part of the core role of finance). Risk, compliance and governance often sit in finance. There are also people in the general counsel and legal team who are critical to enabling governance. The most important point is not so much where it sits, but that it is treated with sufficient focus, priority and prominence, and that the CEO understands that without this capability, they are unlikely to achieve Outpacer status for the long term. In most Outpacers the general counsel is a direct report to the CEO, as obviously is the CFO. I've split governance out and given it its own chapter rather than include it within finance because I believe it's so important to get it right. Rather than being considered as a function, I think it should be viewed and developed as an organizational capability.

Another important point is that there is strong interaction between legal and the risk and compliance team. At the Outpacer, legal often defines what the relevant legislation means for the company, clearly stating what is required of the business and what would be considered as a breach. That is then passed over to the risk and compliance team to operationalize the way the business will comply with that legislation.

Take the EU Copyright Directive, under which the onus shifts to platforms to ensure that offensive or illegal content is not on their sites. Previously, the responsibility to take down infringing content only arose if platforms were notified that it was there. Legal's role is to interpret the legislation and its ramifications, namely that the platform will be in breach and open to multibillion-dollar fines if it doesn't start policing its own content. That is 1 per cent of the journey. The other 99 per cent lies in the operational element of putting the processes and structures in place, how that policing will be achieved, how it will be resourced and how it will be embedded into each product. Traditionally, those operational decisions will sit in finance, but the best decisions will be made if legal and finance are able to collaborate and provide a clear picture of what is required for compliance.

Consultants will talk about the RACI – Responsible, Accountable, Consulted, Informed – framework. This framework lists the people who will be responsible for the work, who will have the final say, who should be consulted and who need to be kept informed. When it comes to governance, having a RACI framework in place that provides total clarity over roles and responsibilities is very important. It doesn't matter if the operating model isn't perfect. It's important but it's not the be all and end all. It's more important to know who is on the hook for what, who should be consulted and who should provide input, rather than spending hours trying to perfect where everyone sits in the business and who rolls up to who. If you have talented people who are clear on their roles and responsibilities, and are aware of the need to interact with other teams, there will be flexibility and agility within the operating model.

Get the right tech

We've briefly talked about the negative image that risk and compliance teams have in some organizations. It's not an issue at the Outpacer, where they ensure they're using the very best techniques, tools and technology to be better at connecting different risks occurring across the business, as well as predicting risks approaching the business in the future. There's never a question of compliance being seen as a second-tier function and not deserving of the agile technology funding available to other parts of the business.

Shifting towards a proactive, predictive examination of compliance risk by using advanced techniques means there is a greater chance that compliance issues will be picked up before they happen, reducing the risk of nasty surprises, which could save both costs and reputational damage. Google is investing heavily in this proactive, forward-looking approach. As Spyro Karetsos, Google's Chief Compliance Officer, says, "Too often we rely solely on historical data sets to provide hindsight perspective reporting. We are now ready to raise the management information bar using advanced techniques, such as AI and modelling, to provide further insight into the current environment and foresight into emerging exposures."

One of the very best tools I've seen (and at the risk of inviting accusations of bias) is the Dynamic Risk Assessment (DRA) tool, developed by Dr Andries Terblanché, the Global Leader of DRA at KPMG. Dynamic Risk Assessment is the key with which those deeper insights into risks can be unlocked. It is an evolution in risk assessment that applies sophisticated algorithms and advanced data and analytics together in a KPMG proprietary (patent pending) methodology to identify, connect and visualize risk in four dimensions. This view takes into consideration risk interconnectedness and the speed with which risks can impact business operations.

Combining the latest in applied science with insights from management and extensive benchmarking, DRA modelling allows you to see where risks can be expected to form critical clusters or trigger "contagion" with other risks. By revealing the expected contagion effects between global and enterprise risks, you can then genuinely assess significant threats.

The other key element is that you "crowdsource" input from the relevant teams – not through old-school interviews, but through an online survey, linked to a sophisticated model that takes input from a variety of sources. The crowdsourcing element is important because it means that when the results are shared, team members know that they contributed to the input and that their opinions were heard.

Another benefit is that individuals will spend a few moments reflecting on the broader environment, where the risks are and how they can maximize the quality of what they're doing. The output is also cool. Engineers respect the digital visualization and the sophistication of the algorithm, and are therefore more likely to take notice of its findings.

Rebrand your risk and compliance team so that they are viewed as high value, not party poopers

If your risk and compliance team are to be treated with the respect they deserve, sponsorship from leaders is crucial. If the executive team doesn't endorse the approach to risk and compliance, no one else will. In the Outpacer, everyone from the top down welcomes and sees the value in an enabling governance approach, and this is often directly as a result of a very strong board and chair of the audit and risk committee operating with the complete confidence and buy-in of the executive team. The importance of their role, experience and connectivity to the business cannot be understated. Although non-executives, they have the experience and cross-industry knowledge to help the business know how to be ready for change that is coming down the line. Outpacers in the technology sector, for example, have a lot to learn from those who have worked in and have experience of sectors that are already regulated and have used that increased focus on governance to their advantage. The value of external advice is relevant to Outpacers no matter what point they are at on their journey. Even start-ups can benefit from having a trusted advisor outside the organization.

The head of internal audit has a direct line to the chair of the risk and audit committee. As a non-executive director, they can be approached directly, circumventing the CEO and CFO if required.

It's an important role and the board should be clear about its responsibility and the level of support that person receives.

To help with rebranding, the people within the risk and compliance teams need to ensure that they're not acting as happy traffic wardens giving out parking tickets and relishing their power of enforcement. This can happen if it's the only way that their role will be acknowledged. They need to be shown the importance of their role by senior management. Outpacing organizations pursue the highest quality, not just the rules that are set. The risk and compliance teams play an integral part in this. They share insights and knowledge that measurably improve everyone and everything, raising the bar on how things are done and constantly looking for ways to be the best. Of course the rules need to be met, but for the kind of motivated talent in an Outpacer, simply ticking the box along with everyone else isn't sufficient motivation. Obeying the rules can sound pretty dull and lacking in purpose. No one ever got inspired by following an instruction with no understanding as to why they were doing so, and consequently no understanding of how it could be done better. Knowing that you can add value to become the best is a motivator. If the risk and compliance teams perceive themselves in this way, they can operate like excellent third-party consultants, independent from the politics, knowing their role is to improve things at speed to make the organization better.

On third-party consultants, and at the risk of further accusations of bias, third-party help is a good thing. Outpacers use professional services firms like KPMG to bring in expertise on topics where this knowledge may not otherwise be required over the long term, and therefore may not exist in a business. But recognizing that expertise is required and being able to take the advice on board and act on it is a key ingredient in an Outpacer.

Allow the business to maximize the risk it takes

Having a clear understanding of the consequences if something goes wrong is a hallmark of the Outpacer. "What's the worst that can happen?" sounds like the kind of phrase risk-takers would use, and can even sound quite cavalier. But if you have the capability to answer that question, it's a great mindset to have. The truth is that your perception of risk is often down to a lack of knowledge, experience or research about what may or may not happen.

Don't put yourself in a position where you fail to do something because you have no idea of what could be the worst that could happen. If you have a clear line of sight of all the likely scenarios, you can get closer to the extreme limit before something breaks. When Sir Lewis Hamilton is expertly racing around an F1 track, his team are fully aware of the temperature of the car, the tire pressure and all the other metrics that are essential for peak performance. They know how far he can push it and when he needs to back off if the car is being pushed too hard. They are monitoring it very carefully so that he can use his skill to optimize performance all of the time.

When we talk about maximizing risk, we're talking about the highest level of talent. You can't take a bunch of elite sportspeople and treat them like the average desk-bound individual doing a workout at the gym on a Friday. They are capable of much more. So the question is, if you think of your talented individuals as a group of athletes, are you setting a framework that would be safe within a high-street gym or an Olympic stadium? By having a clear understanding rather than a subjective point of view on risk, you can allow your talented people to get as close to that limit as possible, and thereby maximize their performance and your investment in them. If you have a group of extremely talented people able to work harder, faster and better than anyone else, don't hold them back.

It's a mistake that's often made in M&A (mergers and acquisitions). It's not uncommon for non-Outpacers to deploy M&A to buy a business that's on a higher trajectory to Outpacer status. It's also the case that often these deals fail to deliver the benefits because the teams can't operate in the new culture and key talent exits through frustration. The root cause of this is often the process around risk and governance that restricts the talent from operating in a way that allows them to perform to the max. The bar has been set much lower than it needs to be for the more dynamic individuals in the Outpacer. Back to the car analogy, it's a bit like putting a speed limiter on Sir Lewis Hamilton's race car because most people can't control their car at over 155 mph. He can, so let him drive it.

So that is the goal and no, you won't get it right every time. There will be things that happen – a global pandemic, for example – that come out of the blue and no one can be prepared for. But if you are running your business in the best way you can, then you're in a more likely position to be an Outpacer.

And remember, investing in a project that fails – even after everything is done to avoid it – is only the wrong thing to do if it couldn't have been predicted or nothing good comes from it. That in turn is always about what can be learnt for next time to make sure it doesn't happen again. It may be that the failure is actually the best thing that could have happened.

Looking backwards, looking forwards

As big tech is discovering, the downside of success is that you become a prominent target. The more power that these Outpacers wield, the more they become the focus of regulators and the competition authorities, as well as anyone else targeting a company with deep pockets and an ability to pay out.

Regulation is already happening and there's no turning back. It represents a huge shift for big tech to accept, given that to date it really has been a bit like the wild west. Organizations and regulators alike were in uncharted waters and, as a consequence, anything went. Today's established and up-and-coming Outpacers are looking at a very different landscape.

Big tech's tussles with US, Australian, Indian, UK, South Korean and EU regulators have been grabbing the spotlight for some time. Now China, who had previously taken a more hands-off attitude to big tech, has entered the fray. Ant Group, the country's largest electronic payment provider, was forced to halt its initial public offering days before it was set to raise $37 billion. Orders to radically restructure the fintech giant into a financial holding company, making it subject to capital requirements similar to those for banks, soon followed. The restructuring is part of a broader government campaign to increase supervision of the financial and technology sectors. Alibaba, the e-commerce platform that owns a 33 per cent stake in Ant, was fined a record $2.8 billion by Chinese antitrust regulators. And twelve tech companies – including China's largest – have been fined over deals that violated anti-monopoly rules.

Talking to the tech sector about facing regulation reminds me of the bereavement curve. While all of the below has happened, is happening or will undoubtedly happen, the longer it takes to get to point 5, the harder it's going to be:

1. Denial
2. Anger
3. Bargaining
4. Depression
5. Acceptance

I have spent time researching other sectors that have been heavily regulated, in particular banking, to see what we can learn from their experiences. According to industry experts, many of the banks fought against increased regulation and found themselves stuck in stages 1, 2 and 3. They wasted huge amounts of time, money and focus. As one expert put it, "fighting the regulator is like swimming against a rip tide. If you keep swimming against it, eventually you'll drown."

Given the regulatory motion of travel, it's quite possible that the tech sector "ain't seen nothing yet". This could be today's Outpacers' greatest challenge – will they be able to swim with the rip tide? Either way, the rip tide is here and they are already at its mercy.

The approach of the very best Outpacers is to collaborate with lawmakers and regulators to explain what they need to be successful, while also listening to what these parties require from them as an Outpacer. There are two sides to the story, and while ultimately the power lies with the regulator, the Outpacer can make their voice heard and try to exert influence. A real Outpacer doesn't follow the standards set by others. They go further and shape the regulatory environment in which they operate.

For those up and coming, that level of operation is the gold standard and may be difficult to achieve without significant market power. However, it is extremely likely that the regulation will open up new opportunities. A good example was the opening-up of telecoms monopolies around the world over the last thirty years. These alternative network providers – altnets – fought against the monopoly incumbents benefiting from the new competitive environment and often successfully created excellent businesses. If new opportunities don't open up and create competition for today's tech behemoths, many will consider the regulation to have failed.

As the global regulators come down on tech, it's time to be ready to lead, to grab the opportunities presented and to create the kind of standards that work for you, your investors, your whole team and the communities you serve.

ROXANNE AUSTIN

Named 2018 Director of the Year, Roxanne Austin has experience and achievements that few can rival, a list so long that I'd run out of space detailing them all! She's the former President and COO of DirecTV, former board member at Ericsson, Target and Teledyne Technologies, and currently serves on the board of Verizon, Abbott Laboratories, CrowdStrike, Freshworks and AbbVie. She has served on eight audit committees and acted as chair on no less than four.

All of these businesses have speed, innovation and technology running through them. They need a strong governance approach, but not one that will stifle the great cultures within. As Austin knows, when the buck stops with you, when it's your responsibility to all stakeholders to get the balance just right, it brings everything into focus.

One of her beliefs is that you shouldn't limit yourself to thinking about risk and governance as a program, process or the job of a department, rather you have to build it into your DNA. Austin's approach is to ensure that the business has a clear line of sight on the small number of risks that can take down the whole business. Rather than having hundreds of risks on a huge chart, you whittle it down to two or three things that, if they occur, could spell the end of the business. But rather than being perceived as a "doomsdayer", Austin guides business executives to think about the organization almost as a living being. To ensure that it grows and realizes its potential, you have to take appropriate care (just as you do of yourself or others).

"You could take the approach that you should wear a coat of armor, and cover yourself head to toe in steel. But if you focus on the small number of things that could be terminal, you'll ensure that you're protecting your heart and brain, which not only keeps what truly matters safe, but also gives you the ability to be agile when compared to a coat of armor!" For me, that's enabling governance in a nutshell.

Austin believes this clarity of thought also helps ensure that you're taking enough risk. She knows that larger corporations can become too risk-averse as they grow. This is precisely when "the ankle biters" (what she calls smaller competitors who can become a disrupter) do something or make a move that you weren't prepared for.

When she's informed of a decision not to do something, Austin's approach will sometimes be to challenge and ask the business, "What's the risk of not doing it?" Firstly, she pushes to ensure that the risk is truly understood, as sometimes a business will say no to something simply because it doesn't truly understand it (which is when the ankle biters move in). Secondly, she will frame the decision in the context of the two or three risks that are terminal to the business, asking, "Are we putting the whole organization at risk by doing it, or are we potentially putting the whole organization at risk by not doing it?"

For Outpacers, enabling governance is not just about obeying rules, rather it's pursuing the highest quality. Austin says that it's key to be aware of and honest about your weaknesses. "When a crisis presents itself, it will be the weaknesses that everyone knew about that will hurt you the most." Part of her role is ensuring there's open and honest dialogue about those weaknesses, and that they are constantly worked on.

The challenge for many is that governance and risk can be overwhelming and not very cool. Austin will stare you straight in the eyes and ask the fundamental question, "What could take us down?" By keeping this in clear view she makes governance an enabler of the mVision, rather than a disabler, stopping the business from being exposed to life-ending risks, while importantly challenging it to take risks to ensure the Outpacer trajectory. Roxanne Austin personifies the enabling governance Outpacer characteristic.

SIR CLIVE WOODWARD

A game of rugby, like any sport, has a group of excellent sportsmen or women doing whatever they can to win. It's a rules-based, strategic game. However, given the physicality and the numbers on the pitch, there are opportunities for players to push what's allowed and break the rules. It's not that different in business. Within a group of highly competitive and talented individuals who have all bought into a compelling mVision, the risk of someone or a small group straying from what's allowed to get the job done is actually higher than you might think.

I picked Sir Clive Woodward as our Outpacer for enabling governance as I believe that he put in place a governance structure that became one of the foundations of the World Cup-winning England rugby team. Sir Clive describes it as "a set of winning behaviors, rules or principles created and agreed to by every member of the team or organization and it is a powerful way to get your teams to write their own set of standards that everyone has to buy into and accept."

This is what I described in the earlier section on "Marching to your own drum". Yes, there are a set of rules that you need to be compliant with, but that isn't the whole story. Sir Clive didn't simply give out the rugby union rule book to all his players! He worked with his team to create the "black book" which documented everything expected of them. It contained seven categories, 35 sections and 240 teamship rules, and was constantly evolving. The team played its part in writing its own standards and all agreed to follow them. The black book offered "a holistic model of building a winning culture" and the players not only bought into it but shaped it. When's the last time you heard of someone describing their governance and compliance framework as "a holistic model building a winning culture"? Never, right?!

When everyone agrees the governance framework is going to make things better, you move from being the "party pooper" on campus to the team that are playing a pivotal role in achieving the mVision.

A great example was the creation of "Lombardi time". As with many rules and standards that were enshrined, Sir Clive would set a question for the team and then leave the room. He would let the players discuss and ensure there was 100 per cent agreement amongst them before they made the recommendation to Sir Clive when he returned. In this way, the team decided that punctuality was critical and that rather than just being on time, they would all arrive ten minutes early or be considered late (an idea taken from famous Packers coach Vince Lombardi). Sir Clive was still the leader, but he empowered and engaged his team in the process. His goal was for the team to be on time for everything, but rather than dictating the rule, he gave them the opportunity to propose their approach, and they went further to set an even higher standard. Genius.

In an Outpacer, there is the same appetite (intellectual curiosity) to understand the rules and operate at the highest standard as there is for an England rugby player to know the rules and standards when they take to the pitch. You can't be good at any sport if you don't know the rules and standard expected of you. You wouldn't dream of setting foot on a pitch without knowing what the rules are. The same must apply in your business.

I believe that Sir Clive created an environment where there was clear governance (rules/principles/standards) that fostered a winning culture, enabling the team to become the best in the world. This is the same approach to take when building an enabling governance framework for an Outpacer. Governance and compliance are not about ensuring no one breaks the rules. They're about complete buy-in from everyone to operate at the highest level of performance attainable.

CHAPTER 9

CUSTOMER EXPERIENCE

What does that really mean?

The customer is truly at the center of the organization. The organization maintains a single view of the customer and uses data-driven insights to predict new customer demands and expectations. Every decision is assessed for its impact on the customer experience and every effort is made to remove barriers to customer satisfaction, improve relationships and engage customers on an emotional level. Employees can articulate the customer value proposition and understand that it is their responsibility to improve the customer experience.

Why is this important?

Exceptional customer experiences are at the center of the Outpacer approach. These organizations continuously strive to excite and engage their customers. This, in turn, allows the organization to build trust, loyalty, brand reputation and, ultimately, revenues and market share. Organizations that offer exceptional customer experiences are able to predict and respond to new customer trends faster, thereby reinforcing their bond with their customers.

You made it! You've got to the last chapter (congrats!) and in a sense I've left the best – the most important – until last. This is where the rubber hits the road. An exceptional customer experience is the ultimate measure of success. It goes beyond having happy customers to having loyal fans who can't get enough of your product. It's a stand-alone characteristic, but it's entirely dependent upon you getting all the other elements of being an Outpacer exactly right so that they all work in harmony. It's for that reason that it sits at the center of the Outpacer framework.

Being exceptional

I believe that an exceptional customer experience is the first and most obvious characteristic of an Outpacer, but it will only happen if your organization has been carefully designed to enable all the other elements I have covered in earlier chapters. To deliver not just a great, but an exceptional customer experience you must have: a clear and purposeful mVision; an entrepreneurial culture, with devoted talent in every role; innovation and collaboration constantly driving you forward; tons of data that you can actually use to understand how to design the best customer experience; agile tech; the funding and support from an excellent finance team; and a governance model that doesn't inhibit, but instead enables everyone to do the right thing by your customers 24/7.

Imagine an amazing restaurant kitchen that is preparing all the ingredients of a delicious meal. Right now, all those ingredients have been perfectly prepared and are in the kitchen waiting to be plated and taken to the customer. How it gets to the customer, the accuracy of the personalization of the order, the way it's delivered, the timeliness, the presentation, the colors and smells and the person who delivers it with perhaps the big reveal all form part of the customer experience and really matter. The dish and everything that led to its creation in the kitchen might have been perfect, but that won't count for anything if the final delivery isn't exceptional.

The traditional high-end CX (customer experience) (such as described in the restaurant above) is not the norm for many Outpacers who deliver in the digital world. Management gurus have talked about customer experience for decades, tracing its roots back to the traditional bricks and mortar human interaction. However, all the principles of delivering excellence still hold true in a digital world. The emotion and feeling in delivering to the customer need to be the same. A digital experience with a human touch that prompts a deeply human, wonderful reaction within your customers is what must happen every time.

And never forget that you're a customer too! Without giving it much thought, you already know what a good customer experience is because you're a customer of many products and you've had many good and bad experiences. Outpacers never lose sight of their own personal experience and are able to put themselves in the shoes of their customers all the time. That intellectual curiosity that we described earlier is ever-present, with Outpacers searching for insights on how the customer experiences a product and seeking to always improve it. That's why they don't just have happy customers, but loyal fans who can't get enough of their products.

The theory of Outpacer evolution

> "Species extinction is usually, though not always, caused by the failure of a species in competition with other species."
>
> **Charles Darwin, *On the Origin of Species*, 1859**

> "Company extinction is usually, though not always, caused by the failure of a company in competition with other companies."
>
> **Alex Holt, *Outpacer*, 2022**

Most people working in business know that customer experience is the most important thing for an organization to get right. The (not so) funny thing is that all too often that myopic focus on the customer somehow gets lost along the way. It can happen for a number of reasons: teams get distracted with other initiatives, metrics point individuals towards other things, and people get too far removed from the customer and have the misapprehension that it's not their job. None of these are real excuses, but they happen all the time. One thing is clear: that loss of focus doesn't happen in an Outpacer. For them, it's personal and they compete heavily to win customers.

Although it's been over 150 years since Darwin developed his theory of evolution – and I suspect he didn't have outpacing organizations in mind at the time – we are seeing customers making "natural selection" and a natural evolution of business taking place before our very eyes. Today's and tomorrow's Outpacers ruthlessly pursue underserved customers who will greatly benefit from the enhanced service they receive, and eat up the prior (non)-service providers. Extinction is already happening and will continue to happen to those organizations that can't change fast enough. My theory of Outpacer evolution is pretty simple: either develop the characteristics of an Outpacer to an exceptional level, or risk becoming extinct. Anyone remember Blockbuster or Blackberry?

Using the right map for CX design

One of the most revealing and important exercises for an organization to undertake as it designs its customer experience is customer journey mapping. It's not a particularly new concept when completed with a one-dimensional approach, but those that add both the customer and employee journey to the map, plus an emotional measure for both customer and employee, discover insights that allow for a truly differentiated customer experience.

Mapping the emotion for both customer and employee reveals that unless both are having an exceptional experience – for example, the employee is feeling confident and has the tools and ability to address the customer challenge – the journey is going to be at best bumpy and at worst terrible. A customer may well have been able to move from desire to buy to successful purchase in three steps, but if those three steps were painful and frustrating because the system was slow and cumbersome, the joy in receiving the end product has already been diminished. What's worse, without mapping that emotion, the organization would assume that the system delivered a successful acquisition. We'll spend more time talking about the importance of emotion and the employee journey later in this chapter.

Other key insights revealed in the journey mapping are the internal hand-offs between different teams (be they human or digital). Making sure they're seamless and that the customer journey continues quickly and to the highest standard is really important. Not only do you need the right people (either to interact with the customer or to design a frictionless digital customer experience), but also perfect process, within the right operating model with agile technology that feeds the right data and information to enable that smooth journey between different teams in the business.

Customer experience can dumbfound wannabe Outpacers and, while emotional journey mapping should form part of the discovery of what is going wrong, the other great insight is how much you are investing in customer experience. It sounds like a really obvious question and one every C-Suite should know the answer to, but it's the Outpacer who is always on top of these critical data points and putting the cash into the things that really matter.

I know of one organization whose goal was to lead in customer experience, but who were instead experiencing sector-leading churn. Following the analysis of where they were spending their money, it transpired that they were spending three times the budget on customer acquisition than they were on customer service and issue resolution. They were spending a fortune selling and not nearly enough serving. It wasn't until the balance was struck that they were able to move forward (don't forget, you get what you pay for).

Building and evolving to serve a clear customer need

Maybe you're the next Elon Musk, with new ideas every day that will rock the world, but you don't have to be Elon to create an Outpacer. A century ago, Thomas Edison thought deeply about what drives invention. One of his famous sayings, "Genius is 1 per cent inspiration and 99 per cent perspiration", is in my view 100 per cent true! Think about the customer problems that existed and were solved through flawless execution by some of today's most well-known Outpacers. While there was initial inspiration, it was the perspiration to make it awesome that made all the difference.

I'm old enough to remember a time when if you missed a TV show, you really had missed it – unless you could program the VCR, the least intuitive piece of tech I've ever used! You couldn't binge-watch your favorite series and you had to watch adverts that were irrelevant to you, as part of a subscription to a load of channels you never watched. If you wanted a good movie, you had to drive to Blockbuster to pick one from whatever was in stock, and if you then forgot to take it back, you ended up with a fine (just me?). The TV and movie business was frustrating billions of people around the world. You didn't need to be a genius to spot this huge, underserved group of customers. That's not to take anything away from the brilliance of today's video streaming platforms. They recognized a problem and solved it by ensuring they designed their businesses with an exceptional customer experience at the center of everything. Once the goal had been set, it was entirely the execution of the plan that set them apart, the relentless pursuit towards delivering an exceptional service for the customer.

Google could see a huge bank of ready-made customers who were being underserved by a search engine that put advertised search terms to the top of the list. Google's algorithm, which instead prioritized the most popular search terms, proved to be a more authentic and honest search tool that customers grew to love. One per cent in seeing the problem, 99 per cent in executing the plan.

There will obviously always be a place for truly brilliant innovation. If you have a smartphone-esque idea, fantastic! But you'll only fly with it if you do so in a way that serves the customer. The iPhone wouldn't be the iPhone today if it didn't have a customer experience machine that was second to none.

For the best organizations, customer experience design has become the means of creating a customer-centric change engine that never gets switched off. For the Outpacer it's become a key business capability run by specialists, rather than a marketing project. These individuals hold up a mirror to the organization, reflecting the customer's experience and signposting the way the organization must adapt in line with changing customer needs and desires. This constant monitoring enables the continuous execution of the customer experience strategy. As companies such as Blockbuster have shown, experiencing "future shock" – an inability to respond to overwhelming change in a competitive timeframe – can be catastrophic. For the Outpacer, the inverse is true. They focus on anticipating disruptive forces that will define the needs of tomorrow's customer before the customer is aware of the need, identifying future trends and rapidly deploying great products and services with a perfectly designed customer experience.

Time for a framework

I honestly believe that almost no one wakes up in the morning with the sole intention of delivering a bad customer experience, but nevertheless, it still happens for a variety of reasons. Leading an Outpacer means that you have to do everything you can to design that possibility out of your business.

An exceptional customer experience isn't the result of hiring people with the very best of intentions. That will definitely help, but those individuals will need the whole organization on their side if they are to truly deliver. For that to happen, a great framework that makes a highly challenging and complex issue easier to digest can really make a difference.

One of the best customer experience frameworks that I know is The Six Pillars of Customer Experience Excellence, developed by Tim Knight and David Conway, authors of *Customer Experience Excellence*. Over eight years, Tim and David analyzed millions of customer evaluations across multiple markets and found six fundamental components of every great customer experience. The Six Pillars define customer experience excellence, which, importantly, means that everyone has the same definition and north star. Their research shows that success at all six pillars is a predictor of commercial success, improving loyalty and advocacy.

The pillars are:

- Personalization: Using individualized attention to drive an emotional connection
- Integrity: Being trustworthy and engendering trust
- Expectations: Managing, meeting and exceeding customer expectations
- Resolution: Turning a poor experience into a great one
- Time and effort: Minimizing customer effort and creating frictionless processes
- Empathy: Achieving an understanding of the customer's circumstances to drive rapport

The Six Pillars are rooted in human psychology and motivation and apply equally to employees and customers. Outpacers are outstanding at the Six Pillars, while the non-Outpacer has a deficiency in at least one, more often several of them.

I've spent extensive time with Tim and David and, while they didn't start out with an intention to define Outpacer customer experience greatness, there's no doubt that they have inadvertently done so. The Outpacers are the ones setting the standards that everyone else must live up to, or risk becoming extinct. Let's look at them in a bit more detail:

- Personalization: Using individualized attention to drive emotional connection. Personalization is the most valuable part of most experiences. The distinguishing feature of brilliant personalization is how your customer is left feeling after their interaction. Do they feel important, valued and more in control?

- Integrity: Being trustworthy and engendering trust. Integrity comes from an organization consistently demonstrating trustworthiness. For customers, what is always at the forefront of their mind is the degree to which the organization delivers on its promises. Trust and integrity are rooted in the organization's sense of purpose. They grow and bear fruit where the organization ethically, morally and socially reaffirms its purpose.
- Expectations: Managing, meeting and exceeding customer expectations. Expectations are increasingly being set by the best brands customers encounter. Great organizations understand that expectations are set strategically by the brand promise, then reaffirmed through everyday interactions. Some organizations show clear intent through their brand communications but fail to deliver, while others set expectations accurately at every interaction and then delight the customer when they exceed them.
- Resolution: Turning a poor experience into a great one. Even with the best processes and procedures, things go wrong. How you recover from these situations is critical. Great companies have a process that puts the customer back in the position they should have been in as quickly as possible. But they go further. Just fixing problems is no longer good enough – the customer must feel great about the whole recovery experience.
- Time and effort: Minimizing customer effort and creating frictionless processes. Customers are time-poor and increasingly looking for instant gratification. Removing unnecessary obstacles, impediments and bureaucracy to enable the customer to achieve their objectives quickly and easily increases loyalty. Many companies are discovering how to use time as a source of competitive advantage. There is also a clear cost advantage to saving time.

- Empathy: Achieving an understanding of the customer's circumstances to drive rapport. Empathy is the emotional capacity to show you understand someone else's experience. Behaviors that create empathy are central to establishing a strong relationship. They involve reflecting to the customer that you know how they feel, then going the extra mile and doing something special for them because you care.

KPMG conducted analysis in which customer experience performance was compared to revenues and profitability over previous years. This allowed for a comparison in the performance of those companies excelling at the Six Pillars (and making it into the CEE top 100) to the main FTSE 100 index. The difference was striking. Over a five-year period, the UK top 10 brands achieved 10 times the revenue growth of their FTSE 100 counterparts.

Outpacers have a preoccupation with excellence at all levels of the organization and the creation of what they want to be acknowledged as globally recognized best practice. They focus on engaging and empowering their people to make great recommendations and decisions for customers, both in person and online. There is a strong discipline around execution so that experience designs are delivered by integrated, well-funded cross-functional teams that prove the financial return of exceptional customer experience time and time again. The Six Pillars have been woven into the fabric of the organization, all working in perfect harmony.

As I mentioned earlier, for many of today's and tomorrow's Outpacers, scaling the business means human interaction is light or almost non-existent. While the framework's conception may predate some of today's Outpacers, its principles – particularly around emotions – have never been more relevant. In the absence of human interaction, it's even more important to engineer a human touch into a digital experience.

To expand on the Six Pillars framework, let me share five ways in which you can ensure that you build an exceptional customer experience into your business and outpace your competition.

WHAT'S THE STORY?

That story needs to be that customers are getting an exceptional customer experience. For that to happen there needs to be a *proper* plan!

Hopefully I'm stating the obvious here, but the customer experience plan has to be an extension of the mVision. To be a successful Outpacer, the mVision will of course be a purpose-driven statement that results in happy customers. The customer experience plan needs to be the detail that sits beneath the headlines with the exact explanation of the who, the how and the what.

As you pull that plan together, there is a tricky but extremely important balance to be struck between profit and purpose. Ultimately, you have to turn a profit, but if you set out with that as your primary goal, you won't inspire the kind of reaction you need from anyone. When it comes to creating profitable customers, you must set economic goals at each stage that everyone can get behind. Excelling at customer experience isn't going to be cheap. Depending on your stage of maturity, it may even mean that you choose to acquire customers at a loss until you have sufficient numbers. Whatever the goals are, everyone needs to be on board and supportive of the way you are going to create happy and profitable customers.

As I've said, customer experience is the ultimate measure of whether you are excelling and all Outpacer characteristics are performing brilliantly. When they are, you have a finance team displaying financial excellence in your corner, wanting to invest for the return they know will come. And it will come. Time and time again, we see the benefits of price elasticity linked to demand for those delivering exceptional customer experience and creating that fan-like following.

The importance of creating a sense of purpose for everyone in the company on customer experience can't be emphasized enough. It flows from the carefully crafted mVision and is reinforced by leadership all the time. Amazon founder Jeff Bezos is obsessed with customers, demonstrated by his mantra: "Start with the customer and work backward." He is famous for leaving an empty chair at the conference table and letting attendees know it's occupied by "the most important person in the room" – the customer.

The key thing in an Outpacer is that everyone cares, from the boardroom to the gatepost. There's simply nothing more important than delighting the customer and having them happily coming back for more. The experience design that you've completed lets everyone know where they need to be and what they need to do.

That design, along with the emotional journey mapping, sets clear expectations of each and every member of the organization. It's similar to the manager of a sports team. That manager will ask the team members to play within a system that's aligned to the match strategy. They need to each play in position, have the creativity and talent to work around the unexpected, and totally commit to the objective to win the game. The structure, focus, discipline and empathic communication are often what set apart great team managers. Outpacers may be a long way from the sports field, but the same approach still gets the win.

Finally, when someone asks, "What's the story?", you need to be able to answer based on detailed measures of your success in real time. Outpacers don't wait for customer focus groups to get feedback on their products. In today's digital-driven world, measurement and performance are almost gamified, with product take-up and feedback across the internet and "in your face" whether you like it or not. As we will see, how you react to that feedback will define your success.

With the overwhelming quantity of data and information, the Outpacer sets the right targets and measures. You can measure lots of stuff, but what's really going to make the difference in your market and to your target customers is all that matters. Once that's clear, you have to flow goals, objectives and incentives 100 per cent behind it. I see Outpacers using transparency to their advantage to both build trust and drive a competitive element to achieving the customer experience objectives across their organizations.

BUILD FOR THE JOURNEY

Your entire operating model needs to make it simple and easy to delight the customer today, while anticipating and preparing to delight them tomorrow. A rigid organizational structure, for example where marketing, product or customer ops teams have an almost siloed responsibility for customer experience, will inhibit your ability to deliver. The Outpacer has a flat, multi-disciplined operating model, so that it can share a single view of the customer that allows input from all teams. Different teams still exist, but collaboration at speed with an agreed view of the customer allows the Outpacer to excel at experience management across a range of products, which in turn creates fan-like responses from customers.

For this to work in practice, you need a connected enterprise. This is the seamless integration of customer experience process flow that traditionally would have been described as back office to front office (or vice versa). Most Outpacers are connected in this way and have the agile technology required to create a single view of the customer. All the information available about the customer through internal, external, big data and social media sources is inputted to create a single view that informs everybody. Increasingly, it is how well the organization harnesses their insights ecosystem that determines the success of the customer experience delivered. Applying the latest machine learning and AI to this data creates real competitive advantage, not only providing a real-time read-out of how you're doing right now, but also giving predictions of what your customers will want next.

Meanwhile, in the non-Outpacer, the opposite takes place. A product manager wants to introduce a new feature for a product and change the pricing, for example, but is told by the back office that it'll take twelve weeks as nothing is connected and it will be a manual lift to get things done. Unfortunately, by that time, the customer is frustrated and an Outpacer leaps at the opportunity to serve them.

Outpacers create the practice of experience management across the enterprise through all the elements of the Outpacer framework. It's as much about your devoted talent and data-driven insights as it is about the enabling governance framework that allows that talent to take the right decisions for the customers.

Building for the journey includes thinking about reinvestment of the profits that come from your success. How will you divvy up the cash generated between new product development and new and enhanced customer experience? It's an important question that needs answering. The ratio between product creation and product activation through an exceptional customer experience needs to reflect back to your mVision. Some believe in letting the product do the talking, but an Outpacer combines an exceptional product with an exceptional experience. Apparently, Apple sets a certain number of seconds that it should take for the box of a new iPhone to open, optimizing the time between frustration and anticipation. The phone is phenomenal, and so is the experience of opening it. The lesson here is that you should let no stone go unturned in the pursuit of exceptional customer experience.

I GET SO EMOTIONAL

While you need a heavy amount of process and structure to make customer experience work, remember that what you're trying to achieve is a certain emotional state in both your people and your target customers. Think about watching an incredible dance routine: it looks effortless for the dancers and provokes an emotional response in you – sometimes even goosebumps or a racing heart.

If I asked you to think about a product you love, you could probably name at least one or two. You wouldn't think twice about me having used the word "love" about a product you've purchased or a service you use. Yet this word conveys intense feelings and deep emotion.

For the Outpacer, the goal is to create a strong emotional response to their product. But like the dancers, this doesn't just happen serendipitously. For them, it's taken hours and hours of structured practice to get the choreography right (and guess what, the perfect routine almost never happens, as there's always something to improve on). That's very similar to customer experience. You have to meticulously plan it in order to get your customers into that desired state and, like the dancers, keep working at it to continue building that emotional connection.

There's no doubt that this is very challenging, but the emotional journey mapping I described earlier enables the Outpacer to take something that can be quite nebulous and make it clear. Hard data allows team members to understand their role and that of specific interventions they can make, then design the customer experience to evoke a desired emotional response that creates a deep relationship between the customer and the product.

For many Outpacers the goal is a frictionless digital experience. Customer interactions may not even be with a human, just a fast and effective user interface (UI). But the fact that it's a digital experience doesn't change a thing. Your users/customers still have an emotional reaction to your product(s) that will determine their experience of the journey you designed. You need to carefully map the emotional experience and ensure that even though it's digital, it doesn't miss a beat in creating the desired emotional response to your product.

Going back to the Six Pillars, you'll see that when done extremely well, they all create an emotional response in the user. In fact, the Outpacers use that emotional response to create a relationship with their customer that goes well beyond a single transaction. In particular, a focus on two pillars – empathy and personalization – pays dividends when creating that emotional connection.

What we've seen from today's Outpacers is that they've mastered the creation of emotion between themselves and their customers. Think about the emotion of losing your iPhone or, for a large group of society, being cut off from social media, not having access to online delivery, or favorite TV shows, or gaming platforms. The reaction can be intense – frustration, sadness and even a feeling of loss.

That's got to be the goal. If your partner decides to end your relationship and your reaction is relief, it's probably fair to say that the emotional connection just wasn't there. You don't want that to be the case with your customers. Being cut off from your product or service should be devastating because your customers can't live without it! And the same goes if they walk out on you. You should take it personally and do whatever it takes to win them back. Use emotion to create a really strong relationship that is the envy of all the competition around you.

WHAT GOES AROUND COMES AROUND

I'm a big believer in business karma – all my experience points to the fact that what goes around comes around! And it's never more true than when looking at the correlation between employee experience and the customer experience.

The Outpacer strives to perform at the highest standards not only for its customers, but also for its employees, making it an outstanding place to work. Outpacers recognize there is an inextricable connection between the experience an employee has day to day and the resulting experience they deliver for customers. While there are outliers (they tend to not last for long or mend their ways), the greatest predictor of an exceptional customer experience is an exceptional employee experience.

Think of it as a double whammy. By treating your employees exceptionally well, you're more likely to attract and retain the devoted talent I describe in Chapter 3, who are by definition highly likely to deliver an exceptional customer experience. So you win both ways!

No matter how caring employees are, or how strong their natural ability to build relationships, if they don't experience that same treatment from their employer or manager, or witness it from leadership, their propensity to act in this way will slowly start to fade. Outpacers take upward and 360-degree feedback extremely seriously. The upward feedback on you as a manager is every bit as, or perhaps even more, important than your manager's thoughts about you. The HR team designing each employee's journey will know that it is every bit as important as the customer journey, and that the values and principles that govern each are perfectly aligned.

Outpacers have moved from the archaic organizational or even military model, which sees employees as people to be controlled and managed, to a contrasting and inspiring culture where employees are to be empowered and enabled. Set the framework, explain the plan and each individual's role within it, then let your talent go to work. You want decisions that impact the customer to be taken as close to the customer as possible. If someone in the team can find a way to make the customer experience better, let them get on with it. An exceptional customer experience is made possible by an enabling governance framework.

Remember the incredible words of Gandhi: "Be the change you want to see." Treat your people exactly how you want them to treat your customers.

NEVER FINISHED

We've talked a bit about continuous improvement and feedback loops, but in reality the Outpacer's products and services are never finished. This is as much about mentality as it is about process. Rarely does an outpacing product manager sit down with their feet up celebrating their great achievement. They will be sitting with the broader team analyzing the customer feedback, spending time thinking and developing the next update or iteration of the product or service.

In Chapter 4 on Collaborative Innovation we talked about the Minimum Viable Product approach (MVP) used in the world's tech hubs to get a product out to market as soon as possible. If you want to deliver an exceptional customer experience, you might think it's best to wait until it's 100 per cent perfect. The problem with that approach is that you will simply be too slow. There's also only so much internal feedback you can get. The benefits of digital are that you can get your product out to market, get the customer feedback and then deliver a software update to improve it extremely quickly. The engineers who are an integral part of the team see what the customer wants and needs and are ready to go like an emergency service!

You may have missed a beat on the initial release in some shape or form, but the reaction from your customers when they see that you've listened and made the changes they wanted to see is often profound. It's said that the Google algorithm is changed and improved at least daily. That team never stops pushing to make the Google search capability better than the last search you made.

Alongside feedback from customers, you also need to use a combination of creativity and entrepreneurial flair, together with predictive data-driven insights, to get ahead of your customers and deliver the products and services they didn't even know they wanted or needed. I love this quote from Steve Jobs: "Our job is to figure out what they're going to want before they do." I think Henry Ford once said, 'If I'd asked customers what they wanted, they would've told me a faster horse.' People don't know what they want until you show it to them. That's why I never rely on market research."

The "never finished" mentality of exceptional customer experience brings together all of the Outpacer characteristics: clear mission and vision, entrepreneurial culture, devoted talent, innovation and collaboration, data-driven insights, agile tech, financial excellence and enabling governance. There are no shortcuts to becoming an Outpacer and no one person (no matter how great!) can do it alone. To deliver an exceptional customer experience you need to combine a drive for greatness and a humility that allows you to listen and improve with an unstoppable belief that what you do next will always be better than what you just did.

As I draw this book to a close, I'd like to emphasize how the nine characteristics are completely interwoven, ultimately leading to the most incredible customer experience, as we've outlined above. The characteristics are like all the ingredients to the perfect meal. A great chef can change the quantity of each ingredient and even how much emphasis they want it to have. That will determine the flavor, and that flavor will be, and should be, unique and authentic to you. When building an Outpacer, the ingredients are clear, but how much focus you place on each characteristic and your orchestration of how they interact will determine what kind of Outpacer you will be . . . and I can't wait to read and hear all about it. Good luck and enjoy the ride!

JEFF BEZOS

Obsession is defined as "the state in which a person's mind is completely filled with thoughts of one particular thing or person in a way that is not normal".

Jeff Bezos will tell anyone who will listen that he and Amazon have a "customer obsession". And while I'll leave others to decide if *he* is normal, I will say what that obsession has achieved is far from normal. It's extraordinary. By his achievements, Bezos amply demonstrates that centering your business around the customer and letting everything else flow from there is the winning formula for a wannabe Outpacer.

"Obsessing over customer experience is the only long-term defensible competitive advantage," Bezos has said. When you get that total focus and obsession coming from the person in charge, the leadership tone is set and permeates the whole organization – it becomes cultural. But, as we all know, that is a pretty rare accomplishment. Nearly all CEOs talk about being customer-centric, but with Bezos's self-proclaimed obsession, he went much further than any CEO I can think of to instill the customer into every thought and decision. Take the famous empty chair in every Amazon meeting, acting as a visible cue to represent the customer. Or the fact that every project or product at Amazon starts with a press release that features imaginary sample customer quotes, highlighting why they love the product. From day one, Bezos built for the journey, making sure that every which way an Amazonian turned, they saw the customer and were forced to think about them first.

Earlier in the chapter I highlighted the importance of building and evolving to serve a clear customer need. Bezos had total clarity on what that meant for online retail: "low prices, big selection and fast delivery". Take a moment to reflect on how breathtakingly simple these three are – they're hardly a secret! Yet Amazon has outpaced every retailer in the world by fundamentally structuring everything they do around meeting these customer needs. Importantly, Bezos does not see them as static – they are long-term needs. Meeting them requires Amazon to bring its other values, such as "invent and simplify", to ensure that it is constantly finding new ways to deliver an exceptional customer experience.

While most CEOs will try to paint a rosy picture, Bezos has a belief that customers are always dissatisfied. But rather than this being a source of pain and anxiety, it's his driving force. His view is that customers want a better way, even if they don't know it. He sees it as Amazon's role to invent on their behalf, knowing that it's not the customers' job to invent or even know what that better way is. That's the obsession: never being satisfied with whatever customer success is being achieved and having that "never finished" attitude, always trying to find new ways to improve.

His obsession underpins outpacing success in retail and in business-to-business through the incredible success of Amazon Web Services (AWS). To succeed in one line of business is amazing, but to outpace in two is almost unfathomable. But that's also the lesson to take away. Everything you do in your business leads you to this central truth: it's all about the customer. "Start with the customer and work backward." Bezos's obsession with customers, along with his commitment to reinvesting profits and focusing on the long term, has created a business that delivers such an exceptional customer experience that it's hard to see anyone catching this – literally – outpacing rocketship!

STEVE JOBS

I couldn't write this book and not talk about the legend that is Steve Jobs. I believe Jobs transcended the business world and became a popular icon because he gifted the world technology that's beautiful to look at, easy to use and makes our lives better.

Jobs had a deep belief that "you've got to start with the customer experience and work backwards toward the technology – not the other way around". Scar tissue from previous experience meant that he knew to ask, "What incredible benefits can we give to the customer? Where can we take the customer?" and not start by "sitting down with the engineers, figuring out what awesome technology we have and how we're going to market it".

In my mind, outpacing at exceptional customer experience is about creating a human connection, understanding and using emotion to positively engage with your customers. At the launch of the iPad 2, Steve Jobs said, "It's in Apple's DNA that technology alone is not enough. It's technology married with liberal arts, married with the humanities, that yields us the results that make our heart sing." I believe this is most certainly at the core of how their products and services seamlessly fit into our lives, connecting on a human and emotional level. I will happily report feeling that connection, and seemingly more than a billion Apple customers feel the same.

Jobs didn't just reinvent personal computing. He reinvented the music industry, animated movies through his leadership at Pixar, digital publishing, the mobile phone and tablet computing. He would be happy that his legacy continues, with Apple pushing to reinvent new industries such as digital health, TV, financial services and news.

Jobs is also credited with reimagining the retail customer experience. Cast your mind back to a time before the Apple store. Buying tech at a big retailer used to be a pretty awful experience, with long waits for often weary, non-expert staff who didn't necessarily know much more than you. Jobs wanted the Apple store to be the best customer experience anywhere. When they looked around for inspiration to bring his vision to light, they headed straight for the Ritz-Carlton. They benchmarked against a five-star hotel and from there apparently learnt about greeting customers on arrival – notice the warm greeting you get now as you enter the Apple store. They were apparently inspired by the concierge desk to create the Genius Bar, staffed with empathetic, knowledgeable team members who are there to help you.

Intellectual curiosity and a desire for inspiration from outside the environment they mostly inhabit lie at the heart of outpacing DNA. It's not guaranteed that it'll work for you, but if you keep your head down and don't look up, you will undoubtedly miss out. In his famous Stanford address, Jobs stated that if he hadn't had the curiosity to take a calligraphy class, Apple would never have developed the beautiful typography pioneered in the Mac and adopted across the PC market.

In Walter Isaacson's brilliant biography of Jobs, he describes their last discussion just weeks before his death from cancer, where they discussed his views on God, faith and the possibilities of an afterlife. He recalls that Jobs wanted to believe that something survives after death. Isaacson then recounts:

> "He fell silent for a very long time.
>
> 'But on the other hand, perhaps it's like an on–off switch,' he said.
>
> '*Click*! And you're gone.'
>
> Then he paused again and smiled slightly.

'Maybe that's why I never liked to put on–off switches on Apple devices.'"

I have no definitive answer for you on an afterlife. But I can tell you that, while Steve Jobs may not be alive today, his genius lives on every day at Apple and across multiple industries where his famous relentless quest for perfection has inspired and pushed the technology in our lives forward for the better. If he did hope that something survives after death, then I'm happy to report that his legacy of bringing products and services to us "that make our heart sing" most certainly lives on.

RIP Steve Jobs.

OUTPACER NOTES

Please note all online resources were last accessed upon the printing of this book in January 2022.

INTRODUCTION

P1 **"Faangs" [. . .] have added $8 trillion in share values:** Wang, L. (2021) 'Sky-High Faang Stocks Were Never Anything But Screaming Bargains', *Bloomberg*, 11 September. Available at: https://www.bloomberg.com/news/articles/2021-09-11/sky-high-faang-stocks-were-never-anything-but-screaming-bargains.

CHAPTER 1

P9 **US "should commit itself to achieving the goal [. . .]":** Kennedy, John F. (1961) *Address to Joint Session of Congress* [Speech Transcript]. Washington, DC: 25 May. Available at: https://www.jfklibrary.org/node/16986.

P11 **"We have a sporting chance of sending a three-man crew around the moon ahead of the Soviets. [. . .]":** Von Braun, W. (1961) 'Letter to the Vice President of the Unites States', 29 April. Available at: https://cdm16608.contentdm.oclc.org/digital/collection/p16608coll1/id/14643.

P11 **Apple Mission:** Apple. (2018) *Annual Report 2018*.

P12 **Facebook Mission:** Facebook. (2020) *Annual Report 10-K*.

P12 **Netflix Mission:** Dipboye, Robert L. (2018) *The Emerald Review of Industrial and Organizational Psychology*. United Kingdom: Emerald Publishing Limited, p. 332.

P12 **Microsoft Mission:** Microsoft. (c.2022) *Microsoft UK*. Available at: https://www.microsoft.com/en-gb/about/.

P15 **"We will continue to make investment decisions in light of long-term market leadership considerations [. . .]":** Bezos, J. (1997) *1997 Annual Report*. Available at: https://www.aboutamazon.com/news/company-news/2020-letter-to-shareholders.

P16 **"I believe everyone should have a voice and be able to connect. [. . .]":** Zuckerberg, M. (2019) *Understanding Facebook's Business Model*. Available at: https://about.fb.com/news/2019/01/understanding-facebooks-business-model/.

P18 **AWS (Amazon Web Services) is now responsible for two thirds of Amazon's profits:** Fortson, D. (2020) 'Chances and Challenges facing Amazon's new boss', *The Times*, 7 February. Available at: https://www.thetimes.co.uk/article/chances-and-challenges-facing-amazons-new-boss-8ghj2c025.

P20 **Google Mission:** Google. (c.2022) *About Google*. Available at: https://about.google/.

P21 **"At the time satellite imagery was quite expensive to acquire [. . .]":** Gibbs, S. (2015) 'Google Maps: a decade of transforming the mapping landscape', *The Guardian*, 8 February. Available at: https://www.theguardian.com/technology/2015/feb/08/google-maps-10-anniversary-iphone-android-street-view.

P21 **Today Google covers 99 per cent of the Earth:** Google. (c.2022) *Google Maps Platform*. Available at: https://cloud.google.com/maps-platform/.

P22 **The mobile app completely blows away the competition:** Cedci, L. (2021) *Leading mapping apps in the United States in 2020, by downloads*. Available at: https://www.statista.com/statistics/865413/most-popular-us-mapping-apps-ranked-by-audience/.

P22 **it is the "most under-monetised asset" at Google:** De Vynck, G. (2019) 'Google's Next Big Money Maker Could Be the Maps on Your Phone', *Bloomberg Quint*, 10 April. Available at: https://www.bloombergquint.com/technology/google-flips-the-switch-on-its-next-big-money-maker-maps.

P23 **"Any decision about a new product or a new hire, I'm always thinking about that sense of purpose and culture.":** Della Cava, M. (2017) 'Microsoft's Satya Nadella is counting on culture shock to drive growth', *USA Today*, 20 February. Available at: https://eu.usatoday.com/story/tech/news/2017/02/20/microsofts-satya-nadella-counting-culture-shock-drive-growth/98011388/.

P25 **Amazon Mission:** Gregory, L. (2019) 'Amazon.com Inc.'s Mission Statement & Vision Statement (An Analysis)', *Panmore Institute*, 13 February. Available at: https://mission-statement.com/amazon/.

P26 **"being true to their values and beliefs" was what counted:** Handley, L. (2018) 'There's a generation below millennials and here's what they want from brands', *CNBC*, 9 April. Available at: https://www.cnbc.com/2018/04/09/generation-z-what-they-want-from-brands-and-businesses.html.

P27 **"It's really hard to design products by focus groups. [. . .]":** Jobs, S. (1998) 'Interview with BusinessWeek', 25 May.

PROFILE SATYA NADELLA

P31 **Microsoft "needed to build deeper empathy for our customers and their unarticulated and unmet needs":** Nadella, S., Shaw, G. and Nichols, J. T. (2017) *Hit Refresh*. London: William Collins.

P32 **"the C in CEO stands for culture. The CEO is the curator of an organization's culture.":** Nadella, S., Nichols, J. T. and Shaw, G. (2017) *Hit Refresh*. London: William Collins.

CHAPTER 2

P35 **Hastings notes how many of today's businesses continue to operate in ways similar to those founded in the industrial age:** Hastings, R. and Meyer, E. (2021) *No Rules Rules*. London: Virgin Books.

P38 **over 400 businesses that have carried the Virgin:** Robinson, R. (2016) 'Billionaire Richard Branson says the idea for all 400 of Virgin's companies came from the same place', *Insider*, 10 August. Available at: https://www.businessinsider.com/richard-branson-says-all-400-of-virgins-companies-were-inspired-by-peoples-bad-experiences-2016-8?r=US&IR=T.

P38 **definition of culture is "the way things get done around here":** Deal, T. E. and Kennedy, A. A. (1982) *Corporate Cultures: The Rites and Rituals of Corporate Life*. New York: Perseus Books Group.

P39 **10,000 of them being "the magic number of greatness":** Gladwell, M. (2009) *Outliers*. London: Penguin.

P41 **"My interest in life comes from setting myself huge, apparently unachievable challenges and trying to rise above them.":** Branson, B. (2009) *Losing My Virginity*, London: Virgin Books.

P42 **"Virgin's first record shop had to incorporate all [the] aspects of how music fitted into people's lives. [. . .]":** Branson, B. (2009) *Losing My Virginity*, London: Virgin Books.

P45 **"Don't provide a musical score and build a symphonic orchestra. [. . .]":** Hastings, R. and Meyer, E. (2021) *No Rules Rules*. London: Virgin Books.

P50 **One of my favorite business books:** Collins, J. and Porras, J. (2005) *Built to Last*. London: Random House Business.

P52 **"what got you here won't get you there":** Goldsmith, M. and Reiter, M. (2014) *What Got You Here Won't Get You There*. London: Hachette Books.

PROFILE ELON MUSK

P55 **"I think it is possible for ordinary people to choose to be extraordinary.":** Dowling, D. (2018) 'How Ordinary People Become Extraordinary', *Entrepreneur Europe*, 3 April. Available at: https://twitter.com/elonmusknewsorg/status/882758499989684227.

P55 **"The thing is no one, especially not Elon, is forcing you to work long hours. [. . .]":** Quora Contributor (2017) 'How Elon Musk Inspired A Culture Of Top Performers', *Forbes*, 8 November. Available at: https://www.forbes.com/sites/quora/2017/11/08/i-worked-at-spacex-and-this-is-how-elon-musk-inspired-a-culture-of-top-performers/?sh=717c1ce0438f.

P55 **"In general, always pick common sense as your guide. [. . .]":** Lambert, F. (2018) 'Tesla Model 3 production aims for 6,000 units per week in June after upgrade in May – ~5,000 with margin of error, says Elon Musk', *Electrek*, 17 April. Available at: https://electrek.co/2018/04/17/tesla-model-3-production-goal-6000-units-per-week/#disqus_thread.

PROFILE REESE WITHERSPOON

P58 **"when people try to tell you to stay in your lane, don't listen. Do not listen.":** Rose, L. (2019) 'How Reese Witherspoon Took Charge of Her Career and Changed Hollywood', *The Hollywood Reporter*, 11 December. Available at: https://www.hollywoodreporter.com/movies/movie-features/how-reese-witherspoon-took-charge-her-career-changed-hollywood-1260203/.

CHAPTER 3

P61 **"Choose a job you love, and you will never have to work a day in your life.":** Confucius (1938) *The Analects of Confucius*. Translated by A. Waley. London: Penguin Classics.

P62 **"Adequate performance gets a generous severance package.":** Hastings, R. and Meyer, E. (2021) *No Rules Rules*. London: Virgin Books.

P63 **SAS selection programme is so gruelling and rigorous:** Sof, E. (2018) 'British Army: What is the SAS selection like?', *Spec Ops Magazine*, June 4. Available at: https://special-ops.org/british-army-what-is-sas-selection-like/.

P64 **"Roger kept a bunch of people who would not have succeeded at Energis from our door. [. . .]":** Philby, R. (2020) 'A lesson in leadership from one of the greats: Hire great. Nothing less will do.', *Chemistry*, 24 July. Available at: https://thechemistrygroup.com/insights/a-lesson-in-leadership-from-one-of-the-greats-hire-great-nothing-less-will-do

P65 **KPMG's 2021 CEO Survey:** KPMG (2021) *2021 KPMG CEO Outlook Pulse Survey.*

P66 **voice recognition systems that failed to accurately recognize women's voices:** Hale, T. (2017) 'This Viral Video Of A Racist Soap Dispenser Reveals A Much Bigger Problem In Tech', *IFL Science*, 18 August. Available at: https://www.iflscience.com/technology/this-racist-soap-dispenser-reveals-why-diversity-in-tech-is-muchneeded/.

P66 **"You are a product of your environment.":** Clement Stone, W. *quotes.net*. Available at: https://www.quotes.net/quote/50892.

P67 **four principles within Amazon's core values:** Gallo, C. (2021) 'How Jeff Bezos Consistently Communicates Four Core Values That Made Amazon A Success', *Forbes*, 11 February. Available at: https://www.forbes.com/sites/carminegallo/2021/02/11/how-jeff-bezos-consistently-communicates-four-core-values-that-made-amazon-a-success/?sh=5b76b9f26e24.

P68 **qualities of a positive workplace culture:** Cameron, K. and Seppälä E. (2015) 'Proof That Positive Work Cultures Are More Productive', *Harvard Business Review*, 1 December. Available at: https://hbr.org/2015/12/proof-that-positive-work-cultures-are-more-productive.

P72 **studies by the Queen's School of Business and by the Gallup Organization:** Cameron, K. and Seppälä E. (2015) 'Proof That Positive Work Cultures Are More Productive', *Harvard Business Review*, 1 December. Available at: https://hbr.org/2015/12/proof-that-positive-work-cultures-are-more-productive.

P75 **Sir Clive Woodward describes how the words of a marine helped him shape the 2003 World Cup-winning team:** BBC News Reporter (2007) 'England train with Royal Marine', *BBC Sport*, 25 June. Available at: http://news.bbc.co.uk/sport2/hi/rugby_union/english/6238540.stm.

PROFILE MARC BENNIOFF

P77 **"Ohana":** Salesforce (c.2022) *What Is Ohana?* Available at: https://www.salesforce.com/video/288760/.

P78 **strong mVision, with clear responsibility to live out and uphold the company values:** Salesforce (c.2022) *Our Story*. Available at: https://www.salesforce.com/company/our-story/.

P78 **Salesforce regularly features as one of the best workplaces in the corporate world:** #3 in Best Workplaces in Technology 2019 and 2018; #2 in 2019

Fortune 100 Best Companies to Work For; #1 in 2018 Fortune 100 Best Companies to Work For; #1 in Best Workplaces for Giving Back 2018; #2 in Best Workplaces for Millennials 2018; #9 in Best Workplaces for Women 2018; #19 in Best Workplaces for Diversity 2018 and #15 in Best Workplaces for Parents 2018. Available at: https://www.salesforce.com/uk/company/recognition/company/.

P78 **"an inspiring vision for successful companies of the future [. . .]":** Benioff, M. and Langley M. (2019) *Trailblazer*. New York: Currency.

PROFILE GRETA THUNBERG

P80 **"Yet you all come to us young people for hope. [. . .]":** The Ellen Show (2019) *Greta Thunberg on Whether She'd Meet with the President.* 2 November. Available at: https://www.youtube.com/watch?v=rsNskDfd5CM.

P81 **her "superpower" and used the hashtag #aspiepower:** Rourke, A. (2019) 'Greta Thunberg responds to Asperger's critics: "It's a superpower"', *The Guardian*, 2 September. Available at: https://www.theguardian.com/environment/2019/sep/02/greta-thunberg-responds-to-aspergers-critics-its-a-superpower.

CHAPTER 4

P84 **In 2012, there were 77 million Blackberry users globally:** Seth, S. (2020) 'BlackBerry: A Story Of Constant Success & Failure', *Investopedia*, 11 September. Available at: https://www.investopedia.com/articles/investing/062315/blackberry-story-constant-success-failure.asp.

P86 **SpaceX has the not so subtle "no asshole rule":** Duffy, K. (2021) 'SpaceX president Gwynne Shotwell explains the company's "no a–hole" policy, which she says prevents a hostile work environment and allows big ideas to flourish', *Insider*, 15 June. Available at: https://www.businessinsider.com/spacex-president-gywnne-shotwell-no-asshole-policy-2021-6?r=US&IR=T.

P86 **Without it, Linux [. . .] wouldn't exist:** Hinkle, M. (2013) 'Open Source: A Platform for Innovation', *WIRED*, 14 November. Available at: https://www.wired.com/insights/2013/11/open-source-a-platform-for-innovation/.

P88 **Facebook's acquisition of Instagram "the greatest regulatory failure of the past decade.":** Nakache, P. (2020) 'Congress wants to curb Big Tech. It could end up crushing startups instead', *Fortune*, 3 August. Available at: https://fortune.com/2020/08/03/big-tech-antitrust-restrictions-startups/.

P89 **"focus and prioritization are crucial given our amazing opportunities.":** Efrati, A. (2011) 'Google to Wind Down Labs Site', *The Wall Street Journal*, 20 July. Available at: https://www.wsj.com/articles/BL-DGB-22827.

P89 **Google's value has more than tripled since:** macrotrends (2021) *Alphabet Market Cap 2006-2021.* Available at: https://www.macrotrends.net/stocks/charts/GOOGL/alphabet/market-cap.

P90 **"innovation comes from people meeting up in the hallways [. . .].":** Toguchi, Robert M. (2017) *The Winning Habits of Steve Jobs*. Bloomington, Indiana: iUniverse.

P91 **"It's best to work in small teams, keep them crowded and foster serendipitous connections.":** Rosenberg, J and Schmidt, E. (2014) *How Google Works*. New York: Grand Central Publishing.

P91 **Isaac Asimov wrote a letter in 1959:** Walker, B. (2015) 'Innovation VS. Invention: Make the Leap and Reap the Rewards', *WIRED*, 12 January. Available at: https://www.wired.com/insights/2015/01/innovation-vs-invention/.

P91 **Amazon first let customers post reviews of products in 1995:** Ante, S. E. (2009) *Amazon: Turning Consumer Opinions into Gold.* New York: Bloomberg.

P93 **the value of this process:** Ladd, B. (2019) 'Amazon CEO Jeff Bezos Believes This Is the Best Way to Run Meetings', *The Observer*, 6 October. Available at: https://observer.com/2019/06/amazon-ceo-jeff-bezos-meetings-success-strategy/.

P94 **"Failure is an option here. If things are not failing, you are not innovating enough.":** Winley, R. (2015) 'Entrepreneurs: 5 Thing We Can Learn From Elon Musk', *Forbes*, 8 October. Available at: https://www.forbes.com/sites/richwinley/2015/10/08/entrepreneurs-5-things-we-can-learn-from-elon-musk/?sh=5c82dc974098.

P97 **research looking at why almost three quarters of corporate innovation initiatives fail to deliver the desired results:** Prats, J. and Siota, J. (2019) 'How Corporations Can Better Work With Startups', *Harvard Business Review*, 3 June. Available at: https://hbr.org/2019/06/how-corporations-can-better-work-with-startups?registration=success.

PROFILE SUSAN WOJCICKI

P101 **Susan went on to be employee 16:** Orescovic, A. (2014) 'Goggle taps long-time executive Wokcicki to head YouTube', *Reuters*, 5 February. Available at: https://www.reuters.com/article/us-google-youtube-idINBREA141Y420140205?edition-redirect=in.

P101 **responsible for the design, innovation and engineering of all Google's advertising:** Nussey, V. (2012) 'SMX West 2012: Keynote with Susan Wojcicki, SVP Advertising, Google, Inc.', *Bruce Clay*, 29 February. Available at: https://www.bruceclay.com/blog/keynote-susan-wojcicki-google/.

P102 **"Half the money I spend on advertising is wasted; the trouble is I don't know which half.":** Wanamaker, J. (2015) *B2B Marketing*, 18 March. Available at: https://www.b2bmarketing.net/en/resources/blog/half-money-i-spend-advertising-wasted-trouble-i-dont-know-which-half.

P101 **start-up called YouTube was outperforming them:** Female Founders Fund (2019)'An Interview with Susan Wojciki, YouTube CEO', 18 September. Available at: https://blog.femalefoundersfund.com/an-interview-with-susan-wojcicki-youtube-ceo-7a9f75a310e5.

P102 **"Our goal at YouTube is to be a platform where anyone in the world can access and share information. [. . .]":** Vinton, K. (2016) 'Queen Of The Very Small Screen: A Q&A With YouTube CEO Susan Wojcicki', *Forbes*, 6 June. Available at: https://www.forbes.com/sites/katevinton/2016/06/06/queen-of-the-very-small-screen-a-qa-with-youtube-ceo-susan-wojcicki/?sh=545f50095940.

P102 **2 billion logged-in users a month, across 100 countries:** YouTube (c.2022) *YouTube for Press*. Available at: https://blog.youtube/press/.

P102 **"YouTube is as much a community product as it is an algorithm.":** Vinton, K. (2016) 'Queen Of The Very Small Screen: A Q&A With YouTube CEO Susan Wojcicki', *Forbes*, 6 June. Available at: https://www.forbes.com/sites/katevinton/2016/06/06/queen-of-the-very-small-screen-a-qa-with-youtube-ceo-susan-wojcicki/?sh=545f50095940.

PROFILE JAY-Z

P103 **became the first hip-hop billionaire:** Hogan, M. (2017). 'Every Corporate Deal that Brought JAY-Z Closer to Becoming Rap's First Billionaire', *Pitchfork*, 27 June. Available at: https://pitchfork.com/thepitch/every-corporate-deal-that-brought-jay-z-closer-to-becoming-raps-first-billionaire/.

P103 **"Picture the pinnacle":** Hello Seven (2011) 'Lessons from a Master: Jay-Z's Advice to Dreamers', *Hello Seven*, 18 January. Available at: https://helloseven.co/lessons-from-a-master-jay-zs-advice-to-dreamers/.

P103 **"when you envision your success [. . .].":** Hello Seven (2011) 'Lessons from a Master: Jay-Z's Advice to Dreamers', *Hello Seven*, 18 January. Available at: https://helloseven.co/lessons-from-a-master-jay-zs-advice-to-dreamers/.

P104 **"you bring the best of what you do [. . .] and they bring the best of what they do to the table":** Oprah's Master Class (2021) *Oprah's Master Class: Jay Z*. 26 April. Available at: https://www.youtube.com/watch?app=desktop&v=MNQH-Kxwx7E.

CHAPTER 5

P106 **Gartner['s] model:** Bocheva, M. (2019) '5 Mistakes When Building Predictive Analytics and How to Overcome Them', *Business 2 Community*, 2 October. Available at: https://www.business2community.com/big-data/5-mistakes-when-building-predictive-analytics-and-how-to-overcome-them-02245407.

P109 **McLaren Applied:** McLaren (c.2022) *National Air Traffic Control Service*. Available at: https://www.mclaren.com/applied/case-study/national-air-traffic-control-service/.

P113 **executives cite a lack of quality data as a significant barrier to value creation.:** KPMG (2020) *Enterprise reboot*. Available at: https://advisory.kpmg.us/content/dam/advisory/en/pdfs/2020/enterprise-reboot.pdf.

P116 **KPMG survey of executives at Global 2000 enterprises:** KPMG (2020) *Enterprise reboot*. Available at: https://advisory.kpmg.us/content/dam/advisory/en/pdfs/2020/enterprise-reboot.pdf.

PROFILE ANNE WOJCICKI

P124 **"Big data is going to make us all healthier. [. . .]":** Distillery Tech (2018) *23andMe and Anne Wojcicki: Using DNA Data to Transform Health Care*, 22 March. Available at: https://medium.com/@distillerytech/23andme-and-anne-wojcicki-using-dna-data-to-transform-health-care-f43b37512dc0.

PROFILE SIR LEWIS HAMILTON

P126 **"I don't drive by the seat of my pants and happen to win races. [. . .]":** Pure Storage (2021) *Mercedes-AMG Petronas: Data Helps Drive Victory in Spain*, 12 May. Available at: https://blog.purestorage.com/perspectives/mercedes-amg-petronas-data-helps-drive-victory-in-spain/.

P126 **"all the data the engineers are studying and analysing":** Hewlett Packard Enterprise (2018) *Lewis Hamilton + Toto Wolf talk with Antonio Neri at HPE Discover*. 30 November. Available at: https://www.youtube.com/watch?v=Q95f4iGqgiI.

P127 **"This year I've been driven not just by my desire to win on the track [. . .]":** Hamilton, L. (2020) *Instagram Post*, 15 November. Available at: https://www.instagram.com/p/CHnStu1slHd/?utm_source=ig_embed&ig_rid=e049d026-89f7-4168-a6e4-825764d1f281.

CHAPTER 6

P132 **agile way of working:** KPMG (c.2022) 'Agile transformation: How does it work?', *KPMG Advisory*. Available at: https://advisory.kpmg.us/articles/2019/agile-transformation-how.html.

P134 **one of the biggest media deals of all time:** VanDerWerff, E. (2019) 'Here's what Disney owns after the massive Disney/Fox merger', *Vox*, 20 March. Available at: https://www.vox.com/culture/2019/3/20/18273477/disney-fox-merger-deal-details-marvel-x-men.

P144 **"In this world, you get what you pay for.":** Vonnegut, K. (2008) *Cat's Cradle*. London: Penguin Classics.

PROFILE THOMAS KURIAN

P148 **world-leading engineering and technical prowess:** Grant, N. (2021) 'Inside Google's Quest to Become a Cloud-Computing Giant', *Bloomberg*, 26 July. Available at: https://www.bloomberg.com/news/features/2021-07-26/google-faces-off-with-amazon-microsoft-to-become-a-cloud-computing-giant.

P148 **took an engineering-led business and place the customer at the heart:** Evans, B. (2020) 'Google Cloud's Big Win: the Remarkable 2-Year Journey of CEO Thomas Kurian', *Acceleration Economy Network*, 9 November. Available at: https://cloudwars.co/google-cloud/google-cloud-the-remarkable-2-year-journey-of-ceo-thomas-kurian/

PROFILE WILL.I.AM

P150 **"[. . .]'I'm going to develop my own stuff and sell it.'":** Evans, B. (2020) 'Google Cloud's Big Win: the Remarkable 2-Year Journey of CEO Thomas Kurian', *Acceleration Economy Network*, 9 November. Available at: https://www.ft.com/content/73f7063e-3e94-11ea-a01a-bae547046735.

P150 **founding shareholder in Beats:** Roberts, D. (2014) 'Behind the scenes, a frontman awaits a payday', *Fortune*, 16 May. Available at: https://fortune.com/2014/05/16/behind-the-scenes-a-frontman-awaits-a-payday/.

P151 **"My mission is to get young people in underserved areas to get excited about technology [. . .]":** GatesFoundation (2017) *will.i.am: Technology with a Purpose #GOALKEEPERS17*. 22 September. Available at: https://www.youtube.com/watch?v=7yt_HVAG0fk&t=8s.

P151 **i.am Angel Foundation:** Understood Team (c.2022) 'Celebrity Spotlight: Why will.i.am Says ADHD Fuels His Creativity', Understood. Available at: https://www.understood.org/articles/en/celebrity-spotlight-why-william-says-adhd-fuels-his-creativity.

p151 **"It's the most creative industry in society today,":** Al-Heeti, A. (2019) 'Will.i.am: Tech is everything (especially music)', *CNET*, 28 June. Available at: https://www.cnet.com/news/will-i-am-tech-is-everything-especially-music/.

CHAPTER 7

P155 **"investors know that one of the key determinants [. . .]":** Cowell, B. September 2021.

P164 **70–90 per cent of mergers and acquisitions fail:** Christensen, Clayton M., Alton, R., Rising, C. and Waldeck, A. (2011) 'The Big Idea: The New M&A Playbook', *Harvard Business Review*, March. Available at: https://hbr.org/2011/03/the-big-idea-the-new-ma-playbook.

P164 **Cisco has completed over 200 acquisitions:** Romanski, H. (2017) 'Cisco's 200th Acquisition— a Tradition of Advancement, Disruption and Growth', *Cisco*, 19 October. Available at: https://blogs.cisco.com/news/ciscos-200th-acquisition-a-tradition-of-advancement-disruption-and-growth.

P167 **"We had no mobile revenue [. . .]":** Handley, L. (2017) 'Sheryl Sandberg: When Mark Zuckerberg first said Facebook must focus on mobile nothing happened', *CNBC*, 21 June. Available at: https://www.cnbc.com/2017/06/21/when-zuckerberg-said-facebook-must-focus-on-mobile-nothing-happened.html.

P167 **Zuckerberg solely used his mobile:** Wager, K. (2019) 'Facebook almost missed the mobile revolution. It can't afford to miss the next big thing.', *Vox*, 29 April. Available at: https://www.vox.com/2019/4/29/18511534/facebook-mobile-phone-f8.

PROFILE RUTH PORAT

P172 **"If you don't invest in the long term, you are literally sowing the seeds of your own destruction.":** Stanford Graduate School of Business (2019) *Ruth Porat, CFO at Alphabet and Google*. 21 May. Available at: https://www.youtube.com/watch?v=tq1kvyC-6ek.

P173 **the budgetary process:** Vanity Fair (2015) *Google's New C.F.O. Ruth Porat Shares Her Vision - New Establishment Summit 2015-FULL CONVERSATION*. 8 October. Available at: https://www.youtube.com/watch?v=Qp37xhkb8n0.

PROFILE OPRAH WINFREY

P175 **"The reason I've been able to be so financially successful is my focus has never [. . .] been money.":** Rampton, J. (2016) '12 busines lessons from

Oprah Winfrey', *Mashable*, 6 October. Available at: https://mashable.com/article/12-business-lessons-from-oprah-winfrey.

P175 **"using TV as a platform to speak to the world":** Stanford Graduate School of Business (2014) *Oprah Winfrey on Career, Life and Leadership*. 29 April. Available at: https://www.youtube.com/watch?v=6DlrqeWrczs.

P176 **do not be afraid to "honour yourself" as that is "your reason for being here.":** Stanford Graduate School of Business (2014) *Oprah Winfrey: Take Care of Yourself*. 21 May. Available at: https://www.youtube.com/watch?v=kfLGR0KYuys.

CHAPTER 8

P181 **"I don't think people are going to take the assurances from Facebook [. . .]":** BBC News (2019) *Facebook rocked to its very foundation, says Clegg*, 25 July. Available at: https://www.bbc.co.uk/news/business-49109624.

P188 **Dynamic Risk Assessment (DRA) tool:** KPMG (2016) 'Seeing audit risks in a new light with Dynamic Risk Assessment', *KPMG Insights*, 14 October. Available at: https://home.kpmg/xx/en/home/insights/2016/10/seeing-audit-risks-in-a-new-light-with-dynamic-risk-assessment.html.

PROFILE ROXANNE AUSTIN

P196 **2018 Director of the Year, Roxanne Austin:** Freshworks (2021) 'Roxanne S. Austin Elected to Freshworks Board of Directors', *Cision*, 26 May. Available at: https://www.prnewswire.com/news-releases/roxanne-s-austin-elected-to-freshworks-board-of-directors-301300037.html.

P196 **former President and COO of DirecTV:** Verizon Communications (2020) 'Roxanne S. Austin Elected to Verizon Board of Director', *GlobeNewswire*, 2 October. Available at: https://www.globenewswire.com/news-release/2020/10/02/2103062/0/en/Roxanne-S-Austin-Elected-to-Verizon-Board-of-Directors.html.

PROFILE SIR CLIVE WOODWARD

P198 **"black book":** Pearey, A. (2020) 'Book review: Clive Woodward still has the winning formula', *Rugby World*, 10 May. Available at: https://www.rugbyworld.com/countries/england-countries/book-review-clive-woodward-still-has-the-winning-formula-109529.

CHAPTER 9

P206 **customer experience design:** KPMG (2017) *Engineering a human touch in a digital future*. Available at: https://assets.kpmg/content/dam/kpmg/uk/pdf/2017/05/US-customer-experience-excellence-analysis-report.pdf.

P207 **Six Pillars of Customer Experience Excellence:** Conway, D. and Knight, T. (2021) *Customer Experience Excellence*. London: Kogan Page.

P210 **KPMG conducted analysis:** KPMG (2017) *The Connected experience imperative.* Available at: https://assets.kpmg/content/dam/kpmg/br/pdf/2017/11/the-connected-experience-imperative-uk-2017.pdf.

P212 **"Start with the customer and work backward.":** Lyons, D. (2009) '"We Start With the Customer and We Work Backward."', *Slate*, 24 December. Available at: https://slate.com/news-and-politics/2009/12/jeff-bezos-on-amazon-s-success.html.

P214 **harnesses their insights ecosystem that determines the success:** Conway, D. and Knight, T. (2021) *Customer Experience Excellence.* London: Kogan Page.

P217 **greatest predictor of an exceptional customer experience:** Conway, D. and Knight, T. (2021) *Customer Experience Excellence.* London: Kogan Page.

P219 **"Our job is to figure out what they're going to want before they do.":** Smith, D. (2019) 'What everyone gets wrong about this famous Steve Jobs quote, according to Lyft's design boss', *Insider*, 19 April. Available at: https://www.businessinsider.com/steve-jobs-quote-misunderstood-katie-dill-2019-4?r=US&IR=T.

PROFILE JEFF BEZOS

P221 **empty chair in every Amazon meeting:** Koetsier, J. (2018) 'Why Every Amazon Meeting Has at Least 1 Empty Chair', *Inc.*, 5 April. Available at: https://www.inc.com/john-koetsier/why-every-amazon-meeting-has-at-least-one-empty-chair.html.

P222 **"Start with the customer and work backward.":** Lyons, D. (2009) '"We Start With the Customer and We Work Backward."', *Slate*, 24 December. Available at: https://slate.com/news-and-politics/2009/12/jeff-bezos-on-amazon-s-success.html.

PROFILE STEVE JOBS

P223 **"you've got to start with the customer experience [. . .]":** 258t, *Steve Jobs Customer Experience.* 16 October. Available at: https://www.youtube.com/watch?v=r2O5qKZlI50.

P223 **"It's in Apple's DNA that technology alone is not enough. [. . .]":** Isaacson, W. (2014) 'Steve Jobs's Biographer on the Icon That Changed Business Forever', *Inc.*, October. Available at: https://www.inc.com/magazine/201410/walter-isaacson/steve-jobs-biographer-inside-look-of-jobs-greatness.html

P224 **benchmarked against a five-star hotel:** Solomon, M. (2015) 'What Steve Jobs Stole From Ritz-Carlton (and You Should Steal From Apple)', *Inc.*, 16 June. Available at: https://www.inc.com/micah-solomon/what-steve-jobs-stole-from-ritz-carlton-and-you-should-steal-from-steve.html.

P224 **Stanford address:** Stanford (2008) *Steve Jobs' 2005 Stanford Commencement Address.* 8 March. Available at: https://www.youtube.com/watch?v=UF8uR6Z6KLc.

P224 **brilliant biography of Jobs:** Isaacson, W. (2011) *Steve Jobs.* New York: Simon & Schuster.

ACKNOWLEDGMENTS

There is one Outpacer you haven't met yet, Natalie Holt. She is the amazingly talented, incredibly supportive, unbelievably patient, gorgeous love of my life without whom this book would not be possible. Some might say that bringing your professional life into your marriage is a dangerous thing to do . . . but as she is a Chartered Business Psychologist and qualified Business Coach, I've got to say I am truly lucky that she did! Thank you for your love, unwavering belief and encouragement – including a number of cocktail interventions – to get this book done!

To Leo and Bailey, our amazing sons, I'm so grateful for your understanding and support. Getting a break from the screen to just hang out or watch you play the sports you love makes me incredibly proud and your commitment, resilience and hard work has been an inspiration to me. Before the wedding and the christenings, there was my mum and dad – a huge thank you for your support and love since day one, and being so understanding when we moved 5,000 miles away to pursue the Silicon Valley dream!

A huge thank you to the brilliant Khoi Tu who made the introduction to the incredible team at Penguin Random House and ensured that I was in the hands of a team whose belief, guidance, support and expertise made Outpacer happen! Led by the awesome Elizabeth Bond, a big thank you to the whole team: Bethany Wright, Aslan Byrne, Joel Rickett, Camilla Ackley, and an especially big thank you to

Jo Russell whose expertise was exactly what I needed. The research was led by the super-talented Will Kelsey and was absolutely invaluable.

In my professional life I've been lucky enough to work for and with people who have a "pay-it-forward" mentality. There are almost too many to mention, but let me list a few and thank those not listed but helped me along the way: Jim Marsh, John Pluthero, Roxanne Austin, David Shaw, Chris Dehring, Jane McCormick, Gregory Thorpe, Joe Gallagher, Scott Parker, Liz Claydon, Dan Thomas, Tim Zanni, Gary Reader, Richard Hanley, Miriam Hernandez-Kakol, Philip Davidson and Bill Thomas. There are also people I work with every day that richly deserve my thanks: Monica Mosis, Amy Carpenter, Aaron Smith, Erin Walsh, Cynthia Carothers and Ly Kowalski. To the incredible clients that I have had the privilege of working with, you will, in line with numerous contractual obligations, remain nameless, but my appreciation and gratitude is immense.

To those who gave me their inputs, ideas and thoughts for this book: Jim Murphy, Paul Cheesbrough, Stephen Frost, Bob Cowell, Pär Eden, Lisa Heneghan, Tim Knight, and Parth Jaharvi, a huge thank you! And to KPMG, who have supported, developed and believed in me while giving me an opportunity to learn from and work with the best professionals in the world – thank you!

To the Outpacers whose tireless dedication and excellence inspired this book in the first place, my admiration for what you created and what you do, day-in-day-out, literally knows no bounds.

Finally, a massive thanks to you for reading and I hope enjoying *Outpacer*. I hope that it acts as a blueprint for your own breathtaking success in the digital era!

INDEX

JOB TRAIN

Alex Holt supports and proudly serves on the board of Silicon Valley based antipoverty charity JobTrain.

JobTrain believes everyone should have the opportunity to earn a family-sustaining wage.

While talent is evenly distributed within our communities, opportunity is not. People have incredible talent, resilience, and ambition, but often lack the skills needed to succeed in today's workforce, and meanwhile, employers struggle to find trained workers.

JobTrain is located in the heart of Silicon Valley, where amidst the prosperity fueled largely by the tech industry there are over one and a half million people living below the poverty level, many working multiple jobs to support their families.

JobTrain exists to help people get to work in successful careers so they can get out and stay out of poverty. Since it began out of the Civil Rights Movement in 1965 with a mission to help those most in need to succeed, JobTrain has grown from providing one typing class to the East Palo Alto community into a premier workforce agency that serves San Mateo County and surrounding counties. JobTrain provides full-time accredited Career Trainings, Skills Upgrade trainings, Job Readiness & Placement, Youth Services, Academic Support, a Supportive Services Center, a Child Development Center, and a Wellness Center. The "whole person" approach of combining career skills, academics, essential skills and support services leads to success. Graduates become self-supporting and thriving members of society, enabling their families and future generations to stay and thrive in the Bay Area.

With the disparities in the greater Bay Area exacerbated by the pandemic, frontline workers in healthcare, culinary, and construction have been among the hardest hit. JobTrain remains strong in its commitment to helping the community through the pandemic and with the economic recovery ahead. New programs, advanced trainings, regional expansion, and the goal of full economic mobility for graduates will strengthen the workforce and help the community prosper.

Over the last 18 months, JobTrain has been strategizing, piloting, and implementing programs for graduates to help them on the path to economic mobility. Programs currently being planned and/or tested include 1) college pathways for working adults, 2) advanced career training at JobTrain for graduates, 3) building partnerships with high road employers, 4) career advancement coaching and 5) developing internal skill set for innovation. These early programs represent strategies that JobTrain believes have the highest degree of likely success, but there are many next level efforts yet to come.

JobTrain has launched a Capital Campaign to expand capacity for the tried and true programs that have so successfully empowered our community to start well paying, middle skills careers. This will require an expanded facility in East Palo Alto that will be known as JobTrain's Center for Economic Mobility. The vision for the East Palo Alto Center for Economic Mobility is a hub where all of the programs are delivered, where new aligned partners can join in this effort, where fast paced innovation and program development will take place, and as a platform for scale and replication.

To support JobTrain, donate today at jobtrainworks.org

As one graduate says, "I will forever be thankful for having the opportunity to be a student at JobTrain. Not only did I gain an entry way to start a career for myself as a Medical Assistant, I now have lifelong support from the entire JobTrain staff and I am able to provide for my daughter. All the pain I endured before joining JobTrain has now turned into power."

Patty Apostolopoulos Rally
Chief Development Officer at JobTrain